Praise for *From Panic to Profit*

"I wholeheartedly endorse *From Panic to Profit* as a real-world road map for structuring and growing a business. By applying the tools outlined in its pages, I've seen firsthand how this framework transforms not just management but also profitability. This philosophy isn't just a theory; it's a practical and effective approach that has streamlined our operations and focused us on what truly drives success. A must-read for any entrepreneur looking to elevate their business!"

—Adam Gibbs
CEO, OTC Industrial Technologies

"In *From Panic to Profit*, Bill Canady delivers a masterful road map for leadership teams in private equity–owned, middle-market companies navigating complex turnaround scenarios. Drawing from my experience leading engineering and product development initiatives in high-stakes environments, I find his application of the 80/20 principle both refreshing and practical. This book provides a strategic framework for uncovering value, streamlining operations, and achieving sustainable revenue growth—on demand and without surprises. Bill's insights, supported by real-world case studies and actionable strategies, resonate with anyone driving transformative change in dynamic industries. This isn't just a guide—it's an operational playbook for executives who want to thrive in challenging circumstances. A must-read for leaders committed to building resilient, growth-focused organizations."

—Mark Parker
president and CEO, Royal Coatings, Inc.

"Bill Canady's new book, *From Panic to Profit*, lays out a powerful blueprint for struggling companies to not just remain viable but to thrive in a short period of time. Having worked with the 80/20 process, I've seen firsthand how quickly this approach can double or triple earnings in twelve months or less. With clarity and actionable insights, Canady puts his extensive experience into a road map that focuses leaders on what truly matters: maximizing profits while minimizing wasted time and effort. If you're ready to build sustainable growth quickly, this book is an essential read."

—Joe Ayette
VP Operations, Western Power Sports

"Bill Canady's *From Panic to Profit* is a compelling guide for executives seeking to cultivate a culture of continuous improvement and unlock their organization's full potential. By focusing on the critical few rather than getting bogged down by the trivial many, Canady helps leaders prioritize high-impact customers, products, and improvements. It's an essential read for anyone committed to operational excellence and long-term success."

—Mark Graban
author, *The Mistakes That Make Us*

"Great book in *From Panic to Profit*. It came to me as specific and actionable, very clear. The beginning grabbed me and put me right in the seat of taking over an acquired mid-cap company in a private equity portfolio, needing a quick turnaround. You concisely and clearly lay out a plan to transform a business, providing details for each step along the way. Your literary references and historical anecdotes make the concepts memorable and vivid. Your books have the clearest and most data-driven approach to making any business better quickly. The results speak for themselves. The heart of this is using the 80/20 principle. You cut to the core of the issue and keep it simple. *From Panic to Profit* provides a clear process and approach to get results for any business fast. These insights and playbook will help any leader drive excellence."

—Bret Snyder
chairman, CEO, and president, WR Gore Industries

"Bill gave me the opportunity to read an advance copy of his book *From Panic to Profit*, and I was hooked from the beginning. Bill has lived exactly what the book covers from start to finish, and so have I in many ways. He references the work of other well-known authors in business strategy and acumen, which I have followed in the past. But *From Panic to Profit* captures what many companies face today, with dynamics like the rise of private equity firms, the focus on short-term profitability, and the need for immediate results. I plan to use this book with my key managers to instill the sense of urgency necessary for delivering above and beyond results."

—Randy Breaux

GPC Group President North America – Napa and Motion Industries

"In *From Panic to Profit*, the follow-up to the highly-successful *The 80/20 CEO*, Bill takes us on the recovery journey of a private equity–sponsored business called Rolling Thunder that was sinking quickly. This real-life, step-by-step guide lays out the tools and processes of 80/20 required to earn the right to grow and reach the desired state of a profitable growth operating system (PGOS). Throughout, he deftly weaves historical and nonbusiness anecdotes into his hardcore business how-to, resulting in an easily digestible, must-read for any executive facing a business crisis. Good luck with the launch!"

—Mitch Aiello

CEO Boyd Corporation

"In this book, Bill combines invaluable lessons with great storytelling, which is rare for a 'how-to' business book. By finding creative examples or analogies from historical events, literature, movies, fables, or even religion, he makes each practical observation easy to read and enjoyable. The end result is tangible advice, learned from experience, that sticks with you."

—Roland Mosimann

president, AlignAlytics, and 80/20 expert

"A handful of leading companies have highly efficient operating mechanisms, strategy deployment methodologies, and talent management approaches fine-tuned over many years, often decades. If your organization lacks such maturity, 80/20 provides a powerful, scalable, and replicable model that will permanently reshape how your business is run in less than eighteen months.

Trust the process, and you will discover the true potential of your business. In *From Panic to Growth*, Bill shares the recipe with compelling and practical examples of successful 80/20 implementations. A must-read."

—Peter Hakanson
president, Bihr European Power Sports

"I recently read Bill Canady's book *From Panic to Profit*, and I found it incredibly insightful and informative. Building on his groundbreaking work in *The 80/20 CEO*, this book empowers CEOs to systematically analyze, diagnose, chart a course, and execute a successful and profitable turnaround in almost any business environment. Bill emphasizes the importance of 'thinking required' throughout the book, and I couldn't agree more. It's the most crucial aspect of applying the principles of 80/20 to business. Earning the right to grow and deploying a profitable growth operating strategy (PGOS) requires thoughtful consideration. The starting point in this thinking process is to focus on the customer, understand their needs, and honestly assess why they choose your products or services over competitors. The new CEO doesn't have all the knowledge and intelligence needed to turn around a business. If they think, or say they do, don't hire them. A one-person show does not produce sustainable results. I was particularly impressed with Bill's understanding that team members possess vast knowledge and experience that can be harnessed to improve performance. Unfortunately, in underperforming enterprises, this knowledge is often underutilized. In multiproduct, multi-market companies, people often work at cross-purposes, engaged in activities that have little chance of generating profitable growth. These individuals are usually dedicated to tasks that don't matter to the customer, at least not enough to justify the cost. In my experience, tapping into this knowledge base and focusing on the vital few products and markets that can make a positive impact will lead to profitable growth, even in challenging market conditions. The PGOS framework provides a straightforward methodology for leaders entrusted with the task of turning around underperforming businesses. As always, Bill's insights are presented in an entertaining way and incredibly valuable. I highly recommend this book."

—Ray Hoglund
member of the board of directors, Marcone Supply

FROM PANIC TO
PROFIT

Uncover Value, Boost Revenue,
and
Grow Your Business
with
The 80/20 Principle

FROM PANIC TO
PROFIT

BILL CANADY
BEST SELLING AUTHOR OF *THE 80/20 CEO*

WILEY

Library of Congress Cataloging-in-Publication Data:

Names: Canady, Bill author
Title: From Panic to Profit : Uncover Value, Boost Revenue, and Grow
    Your Business with The 80/20 Principle / Bill Canady.
Description: Hoboken, New Jersey : Wiley, [2025] | Includes index.
Identifiers: LCCN 2024051382 (print) | LCCN 2024051383 (ebook) | ISBN
    9781394331581 hardback | ISBN 9781394331604 adobe pdf | ISBN
    9781394331598 epub
Subjects: LCSH: Corporations—Growth | Business planning
Classification: LCC HD2746 .C35 2025 (print) | LCC HD2746 (ebook) | DDC
    658.4/06—dc23/eng/20250106
LC record available at https://lccn.loc.gov/2024051382
LC ebook record available at https://lccn.loc.gov/2024051383

Cover Design: Laura Duffy
Author Photo: Courtesy of the Author

SKY10099580_030725

For
My wife Debbie, my best friend, my confidant, my love.
My girls Sarah (plus my son-in-law, Nico!) and Hannah,
who inspire me every day.
And my grandson, Collin, the light of my life.

Contents

Author's Disclaimer

Much that I have written here is based on my executive and leadership experience working with various companies and individuals. In the interest of privacy and, even more, the protection of proprietary information, I have either avoided naming those companies by simply referring to them generically or, for convenience, supplied fictitious names.

—*Bill Canady*

Introduction: The Keys to the Growth Kingdom

Please don't skip this section. This book lays out a set of processes and practices that will grow your business. More precisely, it lays out a set of processes and practices that will earn you the right to grow and accelerate that growth.

So don't turn the page. Not yet.

Because if your business is failing, faltering, or successfully treading water, you need to *earn* the right to grow before you *can* grow. And even if your business is already growing, but you want to make it grow more and faster, you still need to earn the right to grow.

I promise that I am going to tell you how to earn this right. But converting that *how* to *action* requires that you and your entire organization commit to and align on the processes and practices of a Profitable Growth Operating System® (PGOS) driven by the 80/20 Pareto principle. If you are not familiar with 80/20, don't skip ahead. All you need to know at the moment is that 80/20 is a natural law of input and output that tells us roughly 80 percent of consequences come from just 20 percent of causes. Put another way, just 20 percent of your effort is *critical* in its effect while 80 percent is *trivial*.

For now, you need to know that commitment to the 80/20 PGOS is everything and that this is not an opinion. It is a fact founded on

1

experience, and I have the receipts to prove it, which I'll soon show you. Just don't skip this section. Okay?

***

There is a rule so important that somebody a long time ago wrote it out in Latin: *Omne trium perfectum*—"Everything that comes in threes is perfect." If you are Christian, the *rule of three* brings to mind the Holy Trinity. If you are a Wiccan, you know that whatever energy a person puts into the world comes back to them times three. Aviators use a rule of three to calculate the rate of descent in terms of altitude versus travel distance. C++ programmers have their own rule of three concerning class method definitions. Hematologists exercise a rule of three to check the accuracy of blood counts. Medical chemists observe a rule of three in dealing with lead-like compounds. Statisticians employ a rule for three to calculate a confidence limit in the absence of observable events. Survivalists prioritize survival steps using their own rule of three. Storytellers have always loved the rule of three. It's the *Three Little Pigs*, *Goldilocks and the Three Bears*, and *The Three Musketeers*. Sloganeers of every stripe revel in the rule of three: life, liberty, and the pursuit of happiness; stop, look, and listen; stop, drop, and roll; turn on, tune in, drop out; Snap, Crackle, and Pop; government of the people, by the people, for the people.

I could go on. But I won't—except to point out that the United States national government is conspicuously founded on the rule of three, with power divided among the legislative, executive, and judicial branches, which work together yet are opposed.

Without doubt, there is a special mojo in the rule of three. So, here is the rule of three any business that needs or wants to earn the right to grow must not only apply but commit to across the entire organization. Fail to do this, and the processes and practices that you find in this book will produce results at best suboptimal and, at worst, useless.

***

Most of this book is about processes, practices, and the tools required to apply and deploy them. I must state the obvious: all the processes, practices, and tools described in the pages that follow need people to *use* them. All you really must know about *people* in general is that there is no business without them. But about one category of people—leaders—you need to know something more: to lead a business to profitable growth requires not a single standout leader but a triumvirate. They are a visionary, one prophet (sometimes more), and multiple operators.

The Visionary

The visionary is the first as well as the final decision-maker within the organization, which almost always means the CEO. Within the triumvirate and the entire organization, the visionary is the highest authority in the business. They make decisions and issues directives to other executives and managers, who are held accountable for acting on them. The visionary sets the strategic goal for the team as part of a three- or five-year business plan. The goal is almost always a target number. The visionary holds the team members accountable for making progress toward the goal and ultimately achieving it. The visionary ensures alignment of all team members by making commitment to and alignment on the goal and all aspects of the PGOS a condition of employment. To ensure alignment, commitment, and continuous improvement, the visionary conducts regular reviews, always holding team members accountable for the results.

The Four Commandments

The visionary holds team members accountable for obeying **The Four Commandments:**

1. Be on pace.

2. Produce no surprises.

3. Be data-driven.

4. Believe that results matter.

Although the decisions of the visionary must be firm and unambiguous, they are, like everything else in any organization, dedicated to continuous improvement and subject to further decisions that might modify some or all the CEO's preceding decisions.

One entity limits the power of the CEO. In corporations that have a board of directors, the board might operate as a check on CEO authority. More significant for this book, however, the visionary—the CEO—like every other leader and manager in the organization, must be committed to the entire program of the PGOS, including all its practices and processes. This commitment is so critical to the success of the PGOS deployment that it must be clearly laid down as a condition of employment.

Why don't we just call the visionary by the corporate title, CEO? Because *visionary* embodies the essential idea of *vision*. In a company earning its right to grow, the visionary understands the present state of the enterprise and, with imagination and wisdom, leads the planning for a desired future state.

For starters, think Henry Ford or Steve Jobs, but get more specific. I see the visionary role not as that of some soothsaying fortune teller but as a person quite literally with *vision*. Set aside Henry Ford and Steve Jobs and think instead of air traffic controllers. They have an incredibly demanding job, coordinating takeoffs, approaches, and landings at busy airports, continuously monitoring highly dynamic situations with many moving parts, calmly and concisely communicating with pilots, telling them what actions to take and when to take them.

How do they manage this? How do they keep the planes from crashing into each other?

Ask an air traffic controller, and you will get a straightforward answer. They learn to "get the picture." That's what they call it. In fact, they cultivate what the French call *coup d'oeil*, which can be translated as the "glance that takes in a comprehensive view." The phrase is usually applied to military leaders. For instance, Napoleon had *coup d'oeil*, General Ulysses S. Grant had it, and General George S. Patton had it: an ability to take in, at a glance, a vast dynamic battlefield. It is a moving picture, and every successful air traffic controller has this get-the-picture *coup d'oeil* ability to comprehend the situation and act on it in real time. Aided by sophisticated radar, they create in their mind's eyes real-time visions revealing each aircraft in relation to every other aircraft within a certain space. Every decision made and every instruction given to each pilot is formulated and communicated within the frame of the picture. The required visionary faculty of a PGOS-driven CEO is vividly analogous to that of an air traffic controller.

Now, because all the parts of the business picture are, like the planes approaching and departing the airport, always in motion, the visionary must be super agile and ultra-focused. Deploying a strategic business plan within the guardrails of the processes and practices we call PGOS transforms static strategy into dynamic deployment. The relentlessly running clock certainly creates pressure on the visionary, but it also means that the visionary's outlook cannot be of some imagined static *state of perfection* but must be a real-life *process of progress* toward a goal, which, like everything else, is subject to revision in the face of reality.

Introduction: The Keys to the Growth Kingdom

The Prophet

The first company I was hired to run (by the private equity firm that had purchased it) was a conglomerate of decentralized businesses sprawled out over diverse markets—medical, technical, and industrial.

In theory, 80/20 guided the entire conglomerate. In practice, unit presidents generally went their own way. At first, I brought in outside consultant trainers to drill 80/20 and related processes and practices into our bundle of businesses. They were good consultants and competent trainers. But they were making painfully slow progress, during which the conglomerate limped along, the ongoing victim of suboptimization. That is when I realized that we needed to internalize 80/20 and our other aligned processes. The only way to do this efficiently and on pace was to bring it all, the whole program, totally in-house.

What did we need? A prophet!

Like the CEO visionary, the prophet is a leader—often, but not necessarily, the chief operating officer (COO)—with the knowledge and know-how needed to deploy the vision of the visionary. The prophet (or *prophets*, because there might be more than one) translates the vision into actions, typically through training, coaching, and mentoring others throughout the organization in the deployment of the company strategy.

More specifically, the prophet is expert in the deployment of PGOS processes, especially 80/20 analysis and execution. The prophet owns the PGOS training of the team, ensuring that everyone understands how 80/20 and other key processes work. Indeed, the prophet is responsible for *training the trainers*. The objective is to develop an internal cadre of PGOS experts capable of training all team members in the key processes. Often, outside consultants initially serve in the prophet role, inculcating PGOS and 80/20 into the team leaders; however, it is impractical to rent a prophet from a consulting or training company for the long term. Without a prophet who is organic to the organization, your executives, managers, and other key personnel will inevitably regress from aligning on the strategy to drifting from it. Without a prophet, they will implement what makes them comfortable or what they individually believe is right. The result? In place of the possibility of growth will be the disorder of suboptimization. If a prophet (or prophets) are organic to the organization, substantial progress toward the goal set for the business plan is seen within three to five months. If no organic prophet is available, significant performance improvement is likely to take eighteen months.

The ideal prophet is not only thoroughly versed in 80/20 and other aspects of PGOS but has led deployment of 80/20 multiple times. If the prophet role begins as an outside consultant—because no prophets are available in the company—the visionary needs to plan a transition from reliance on outside consultants to a fully functioning prophet leadership role (usually assigned to the COO) within two years. Starting from zero, you will need at minimum eighteen months to "grow" at least one prophet in the company.

In religion, a prophet is a propagator of the faith. The unifying structuring principle of a company committed to the practices and processes of the PGOS does resemble a religion in at least one aspect, namely, commitment to a gospel. Call it "the gospel according to Pareto." Religions are generally based on the notion that there is only *one right way*. Similarly, PGOS holds that the only *right way* to embrace a strategy that focuses on the most profitable products and customers is by over-resourcing the roughly 20 percent of customers and products that create roughly 80 percent of the company's revenue.

Most religions rely for validation on faith rather than on proof. The Pareto principle—which we explain and demonstrate throughout this book—offers ample proof and asks for no faith whatsoever. It has the receipts, and it shows them. Consider, for instance, the example of a company that has mastered the use of 80/20 thinking, Illinois Tool Works (NYSE: ITW). In the early 1980s, ITW faced rising costs and decreasing profitability. In response, company leadership decided to use the 80/20 principle to drive a complete overhaul of its policies, processes, and rules of operation. Over twenty-five years, ITW not only perfected how it applied the 80/20 rule but also enjoyed annual shareholder returns of 19 percent without fail—many times by acquiring companies and applying the principles of 80/20 to them. That's one profitable gospel!

Don't have twenty-five years to perfect your practices and processes?

One thing ITW discovered is that profitable growth accelerated pretty much in proportion to the degree that the visionary, the prophet, and (as we are about to see) the operators were all embedded in the company. The leaders of rapid growth were internal, organic to the organization. As mentioned, an external prophet or team of prophets is often initially hired as an outside consultant, but the sooner the lessons are learned and the role of prophet is brought in-house, the better. For, the prophet in a PGOS-driven enterprise must preach from a total understanding of the core strategy and coordinated engagement with the other true believers in the company. The prophet is not the author of the holy writ, however. That is the role of the visionary. No, the province of the prophet is the keeper, the interpreter, and the evangelist of the vision.

The Operator

The operator is the leader who runs the business on a day-to-day level. Typically, there are several of these operators who are operational leaders within the business, employees who hold the company or business unit title of president. In some cases, operators might be designated members of the CEO's staff. In the kind of conglomerated businesses I have run during my career, the operators have been the presidents of segments or of operating companies. The operators are charged with owning, developing, and setting the strategy within their companies, business units, or segments to deliver the strategic goal set by the visionary. Although operators might not be experts in PGOS and 80/20, they understand the principles and processes involved. They must adhere to what I call The Four Commandments, which are the keys to the successful execution of the strategy. Accordingly, they must continuously upgrade and improve their teams to ensure conformity with The Four Commandments.

The operators know their companies, but they are not the source of the overall strategy. That is the role of the visionary. Nor are they the keepers and masters of the practices and processes by which that strategy is implemented. This is the domain of the prophet. What they do have is intimate working knowledge of their companies or business units, and they are themselves thoroughly evangelized on the strategic vision and on the processes and practices necessary to ensure that their business is perfectly aligned with the strategy and meets or exceeds all its strategic goals.

Show Us Your Receipts

What can you expect from applying 80/20 in the PGOS? I believe that ITW was in fact the first business to use 80/20 analysis in a systematic and systemic whole-of-company program to earn the right to grow, to exercise that right, and to grow. The company called it the 80/20 Front-to-Back Process. ITW began operating under the first iteration of this process in 1985. At the time, the company's compound annual growth rate (CAGR) was essentially on par with the S&P 500.

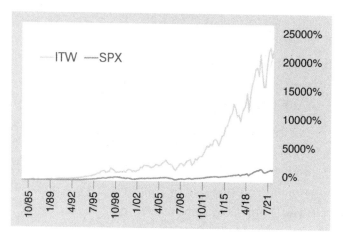

Figure I-1 International Tool Works Versus S&P 500

This performance improved slowly through the early 1990s. Beginning in 1994, a dramatic climb commenced. By 2022, ITW's operating margin was 23.8 percent, compared to 15.9 percent in 2012. Overall, since embracing an 80/20 growth system, the company's compound annual shareholder return stood at 15.2 percent and delivered ten-times cumulative return versus 8.4 percent for the S&P 500 over that same period (see Figure I-1).

The examples of two more companies, IDEX Corporation and Modine, show similar performance, but for these firms we have an added data point, which provides a critical insight. Take a look at the performance of IDEX versus S&P 500 between the start of 2009 and the end of 2023 (Figure I-2).

The 80/20-based process was introduced at the start of 2009 by a team of *outside consultants*. Their engagement lasted into July 2012, during which shareholder return increased essentially on par with that of the S&P 500. During July 2012, the external consultants were replaced by a 100 percent internal team. IDEX had committed to the rule of three, aligning internal leaders—the visionary, the prophet, and the operators—on the 80/20-driven

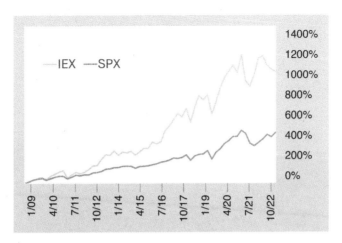

Figure I-2 IDEX Versus S&P 500

processes and practices of the company's growth strategy. The result was dramatic, as can be seen by how sharply the performance of IDEX suddenly veers upward from that of the S&P 500. *This growth occurred only after the company was fully aligned on the strategic execution of 80/20 through an internal team led by internal rule of three leaders.* For nearly three years, under external consultants, IDEX shareholder value was up about 100 percent, only slightly more than the S&P 500. The outside consultants were doubtless *necessary*, but they were not *sufficient*, and they likely remained too long. After four years under internally led deployment, however, with the company fully aligned on the 80/20 growth strategy, it was up a cumulative 400 percent, while the S&P was about 200 percent.

In the case of Modine, 80/20-driven deployment of PGOS began with the CEO and board of directors, and the full rule of three leadership team fully committed and aligned. True, 80/20 experts were hired from the outside as initial consultants, but the strategy and implementation were organic, internal, and the product of total commitment. Figure I-3 shows the result.

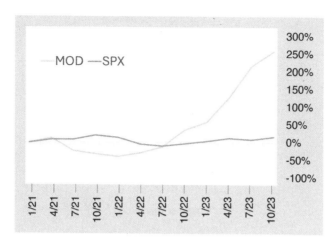

Figure I-3 Modine Versus S&P 500

In just eighteen to twenty-four months, between January 2021 and October 2022, the company began a sharp upward inflection, putting a lot of mileage between itself and a comparatively flat S&P 500. By October 2023, growth rate was up a cumulative 250 percent, while the S&P lolled along with gains hovering just above zero percent.

Examine the receipts, and you discover that your choices are stark:

EITHER commit to earning the right to grow by creating a totally embedded, organic, internal leadership triumvirate in conformity with the rule of three: visionary, prophet(s), and operators. Align the three leaders on processes and practices to build and execute an 80/20-driven strategy. Enable total alignment with these processes and practices, *make the alignment a condition of employment*, and put the company on a trajectory of rapid growth—just eighteen to twenty-four months to your goal—as measured against its own past and present performance as well as the index of the S&P 500.

OR change nothing about your internal leadership. Ignore the rule of three. Embed nobody. Just hire a team of consultants to tell you what to do. If those consultants are really good, you might improve performance, but anything resembling significant improvement will take at least a decade.

Where There Is No Vision, the People Perish

A proverb is an adage or traditional saying that expresses a truth based on experience and/or common sense. The Old Testament features a whole "Book of Proverbs," including this one (Proverbs 29:18–19), which begins, "Where there is no vision, the people perish . . ."

In a business run on the 80/20-driven PGOS, the visionary provides the vision, the prophet leads the execution or deployment of the vision, and the operators act on that vision and its deployment at the level of their individual business units. Although outside experts are typically consulted when introducing 80/20 to the organization, none of the commitment to 80/20-driven PGOS is imported. Sooner or later, all must be made internal, integral, and organic to the business—and, based on the typical growth curves, sooner is far preferable to later.

PGOS will deliver extraordinary results only if the complete triumvirate—visionary, prophet(s), and operators—is present, active, aligned in the organization, and thoroughly committed. The prophet guides the execution of the vision throughout the organization, aligning the company on the strategy and applying 80/20. Without a visionary, however, there can be no vision. Without a vision, there can be no prophet or prophets. The operators take their direction from the visionary and apply it with the prophet's instruction, guidance, and mentoring. Without the committed and aligned operators, the work of the visionary and the prophet comes to nothing.

The homeliest and most practical illustration of the rule of three in leading an enterprise is the humble joint stool. *It requires all three of its legs to stand.* Without the visionary (often but not always the CEO), the team would not have a clear goal. Everyone would be firing unaimed arrows, which never miss yet hit who knows what. Without the prophet, the team lacks a clear map to the visionary's goal. Without the operators, neither the visionary nor the prophet will have anything to do.

The PGOS system outlined in the pages that follow is a set of processes and practices, along with the tools necessary to their execution, all of which foster a common culture, creating value for all stakeholders: customers, employees, suppliers, and shareholders. Under the leadership of visionary, prophet(s), and operators, PGOS enables business owners and management teams to identify challenges to their operations and to create clear, simple, actionable plans to increase the productivity of assets, increase profits, and make better decisions at every level of an organization.

If the organization is fully aligned on the system, it works. If not, it fails. In my companies, *full alignment is a requirement of employment.* That is how important it is. Now, dear reader, you may turn the page.

Chapter 1

Panic

When in danger or in doubt, run in circles, scream and shout.
—Herman Wouk, *The Caine Mutiny*, 1951

Rolling Thunder Engineered Parts—that's what we'll call it—is a large distributor of aftermarket parts for a diverse range of vehicles, from motorcycles and ATVs to outdoor power equipment to heavy-duty trucks. It covers the United States, Canada, United Kingdom, Italy, Germany, France, Belgium, Netherlands, Sweden, Argentina, India, China, and Pakistan. It has expanded in terms of markets, products, and geographical presence. The one thing lacking in all this has been an overall strategy. Growth in and of itself is neither good nor bad. It just *is*. *Strategic* growth, which should be thought of as a synonym for *profitable* growth, is always good. In fact, it is the goal of any business aiming for financial success.

So, for some time now, Rolling Thunder has been rolling flat and down. A recent moment in its history was marked by declining financial results. For the year's first quarter, normalized revenue was down and normalized earnings before interest, taxes, depreciation, and amortization (EBITDA) down even more. Judging from April sales, the trend was not turning around.

Bad luck?

I refuse to answer that question on the grounds that it might tend to piss me off. Branch Rickey, one of early Major League Baseball's greatest managers and executives, the man who developed the farm system and, even more important, broke the MLB color barrier when he risked it all to hire Jackie Robinson for the Brooklyn Dodgers in 1945, said, "Luck is the residue of design." This oracular sentence was his refusal to surrender to the lottery of chaos. It reminds me of something Louis Pasteur, conqueror of rabies and father of bacteriology, said about discovery. "In the fields of observation," he told students at the University of Lille in 1854, "chance favors only the prepared mind." So, don't talk to me about luck. If you feel that you are fresh out of luck, start making some of your own. (This book will show you how.)

You need to look behind the bad numbers. That's what I did at Rolling Thunder. A lot of projects and initiatives were under way. Well, isn't that a good thing? Without strategic consideration of return on investment, it is not. And not without situational awareness of cash flow. In fact, financial data, analytics, key performance indicators (KPIs), and tracking capabilities at Rolling Thunder ranged from inadequate to nonexistent. Tax issues, including add-back limitations, severance obligations, and contractual cash requirements, were all contributing to an increasingly tight cash situation. As things were going, there were not very many levers available for the pulling.

The people in this company were neither stupid nor lazy. Quite the contrary. They were intelligent and hardworking. Their problem was that they hadn't been paying attention, not to the business and not to each other. Some were pulling, some were pushing, and some were struggling just to stand in place. They had not *prepared* their minds, and consequently, the company lacked alignment.

I work for a private equity firm, and Rolling Thunder was one of their new acquisitions. Now, different people go into business for different reasons. Some have a passion for a particular product or industry. Some have a family tradition to honor. Some have certain moral or philanthropic motives. But private equity just wants to make money. That is not as one-dimensional or as crass as it sounds. They want to buy a company low, grow it in value, then sell it high. Done right, private equity makes money by adding significant, even immense, value to the companies they acquire. This is the practice of capitalism at its most productive and beneficial. So, when my firm put me in Rolling Thunder as CEO, my assignment was simple—by which I do not mean easy. It was simple because the task could be expressed in a single, short, imperative sentence: *Turn it around.*

What to Do First

Wait. Pardon me. I just lied. The three-word imperative sentence was not enough, never was enough, and could never be enough. A subordinate clause was and always is also necessary: *Turn it around until it is positioned to earn the right to grow.*

The thing is, when you walk into a situation in which a lot is going on uncontrolled and in all directions, it's natural to get overwhelmed by panic and despair, a combination that creates confusion, breeds pessimism, dissolves morale, and brings on paralysis.

I read a lot and not just business books. I like history. I find it fascinating and full of lessons, examples, and precedents. Political and military history bristles with leadership lessons, and because my profession, as a CEO, is leadership, I'm always hungry for great leadership stories. Take General George S. Patton, the most successful land commander of World War II. His first assignment in that war was to lead the Western Task Force in Operation TORCH, the US landings in Nazi- and fascist-occupied North Africa, which took place on November 8, 1942. These would be the American forces' first foothold in enemy-controlled country, the first step in the eventual liberation of Europe. Early the next year, Patton was promoted from command of the Western Task Force to take over the US II

Corps, replacing General Lloyd R. Fredendall, who had led II Corps to a humiliating defeat at Kasserine Pass, a two-mile wide gap in the Atlas Mountains of Tunisia. This was the very first combat between the US Army and the justly feared German Afrika Korps under the command of another World War II icon, General Erwin Rommel, the infamous Desert Fox. The blow to the American military's confidence threatened to be crippling. A lot had gone wrong, revealing that a lot was wrong with II Corps. How do you make it right? That was Patton's immediate task. To a casual observer, however, it looked like so much had gone wrong that how could anyone even know where to start?

Patton began as soon as he walked into II Corps headquarters for the first time. What he beheld was a dispirited group of men—sloppy and unsoldierly, more rabble than army. He didn't blame the men. He didn't curse his bad luck at being saddled with a disgruntled mob. Instead, he immediately sized up the problem as one of leadership and management. Based on that single conclusion, he knew what to do first. And knowing *that* is pretty much everything, because knowing what to do first—and then doing it—leads to knowing what to do next and so on and on. Knowing what to do first is the beginning of a *process*, useful, productive action toward a strategic goal.

What to do first?

Patton did what he *could immediately* do, which was to address the situation he saw before his own eyes. He knew he needed to institute a demanding regime aimed at achieving "perfect discipline," which he considered the *only* form of discipline. His first orders concerned enforcing Army regulations governing uniforms, including the wearing of neckties, leggings, and helmets. At first, the troops were bewildered. What did knotting a necktie have to do with defeating the Desert Fox? Well, General Omar N. Bradley, who was Patton's second-in-command over II Corps, understood. "Each time a soldier knotted his necktie," Bradley wrote, "threaded his leggings, and buckled on his heavy steel helmet, he was forcibly reminded that Patton had come to command the II Corps, that the pre-Kasserine days had ended, and that a tough new era had begun." Like Patton, Bradley saw the "necktie order" as the first step toward making the men of II Corps feel like soldiers so that they would act like soldiers. In a remarkably short time, Patton transformed II Corps into a winning organization.

I'm not General Patton. I couldn't get away with behaving like General Patton. Fortunately, I don't want to be General Patton, and I don't need to be. But, like Patton, faced with a suboptimal and disheartened organization, I had to begin to *turn it around,* so that it would be positioned *to earn the right to grow.*

Like Patton, I never blamed the people I was tasked with leading. What I saw was a problem of leadership and management. I therefore addressed that. I did what I always do when I take up the reins of a company. I walked around, I looked at what was going on, and, most of all, I asked questions. Then I shut up and listened to the answers. When you are called on to turn a company around, you are inevitably torn in two opposite directions. On the one hand, you are supposed to come in with all the answers. On the other hand, if you are convinced that you have all the answers, you won't learn anything about the company you are expected not only to save but also to profitably grow. If you think you already know it all, you won't be inclined to look and listen, to make yourself understand the culture of the company, to learn about its history, its processes, and its expectations. You won't be ready to learn about its people.

Core Meeting and Open Letter

Very soon after I took my place as CEO, I held the first core meeting—a meeting with the executive leadership team (ELT).

21

Panic

I asked more questions of upper management, and then, together, we set a five-year goal.

Now, you would think that setting a five-year goal would require weeks if not months of labor. Me? I gave it ten days out of the first hundred days of my tenure as CEO. I could do that because I was armed with the advantage of working for a private equity firm. Private equity typically operates by a rule of thumb, which sets as a goal getting at least a three-times multiple on invested cash, so this meant that setting our goal required just five steps:

1. Gather and analyze the necessary data to determine our current EBITDA.

2. Multiply the EBITDA by the anticipated exit multiple to get the total sell price.

3. Take this total and subtract all debt to arrive at the total equity.

4. Divide the total equity by the original equity that was invested.

5. If this number is three times or greater, then 100 percent of your equity vests (assuming your contract vested at three times).

These five steps were accomplished in the core meeting with the ELT. Almost immediately after that meeting, I convened the first company-wide town hall. In this case, it was a combined in-person meeting and a virtual meeting, because it involved some fourteen hundred participants distributed over more than forty locations nationwide and even worldwide. The town hall did not materialize out of thin air. Its foundation was the product of our core meeting, a product I presented in an open letter to all the personnel of Rolling Thunder:

Dear Thunderers:

I am enjoying learning about our business, its people, and its processes. I plan to periodically hold virtual town halls with all of you to share progress updates and take questions. In a few days, you will receive your invitation to our first town hall. Before then, however, I'd like to share a bit about:

1. Where we are now;

2. Where we are going; and

3. How we will get there.

Today—now—our company is missing sales targets, and our costs are increasing. We must take immediate action to remedy this to steady the company. This means quickly cutting spending and stopping all initiatives that are not tied to revenue generation. We will do this, however, not for the sake of making cuts, but to enable us to laser focus exclusively on the most important priorities for our success. Over the next few days, weeks, and months, we will implement many changes to secure our company's health.

I can tell you now that these changes will be tied to my four-step system, which takes about a hundred days to complete:

- **Step 1: Get a goal.**

  This step has already been completed by our executive leadership team. Our new organizational goal is to reach $2.5 billion in revenue, have high teens margins and $300 million in EBITDA by this time five years from now. To achieve this goal, we must first *earn the right to grow.* This begins by *simplifying our business.* The executive team has already reviewed what to immediately stop, what to start, and what to continue doing to get a solid foundation under our feet. We will communicate this to you shortly. Additionally, we will kick off our *80/20 process* by using accurate, timely data to determine precisely where to simplify and grow the business by determining where to raise prices to increase our bottom line.

- **Step 2: Frame the strategy.**

  The executive leadership team (ELT) will reconvene in May to build a strategy that will allow us to achieve our new goal. We'll separate what's working from what isn't and create a straightforward approach.

- **Step 3: Build the structure.**

  We'll organize our businesses in segments to provide focus on customers, new product development, and hitting our goal. The segments will then be organized with a clear structure and accountability to deliver on our goals.

- **Step 4: Launch the action plan.**

  We'll define the tactics and efforts needed to execute the plan. We won't wait for perfection here. We'll make sound, informed decisions and go.

I'm confident we'll be well positioned to achieve our goal by following this four-step system, and I will be transparent in our updates. While we work through this process, I'm counting on each of you to keep doing your jobs, provide excellent customer service, and remain focused on achieving our goal.

After spending the last few days with the leadership team, we all left energized and ready to roll up our sleeves and get back to basics.

We will create something extraordinary here, and I ask that you join me for the ride.

Bill Canady

CEO

Executive Leadership Team Meeting

Preceding the first town hall was my off-site meeting with the ELT, which spanned three and a half days, beginning with process overview and kickoff, a financial overview, and a situational assessment, all on day one. Day two consisted of reviews of each segment within the company, with a specific manager responsible for delivering each review. Day three focused on the application of 80/20 (half day). Day four began with a review of *stop*, *start*, and *continue* decisions before going on to goal formation. After this, it looked ahead to further developing the five-year strategy and ended with a presentation of financial expectations.

The entire event included well-organized financials relating to EBITDA, sales, revenue, working capital, and cash flow/net debt. These financial headlines were meant to serve as a transition from the first hundred days to the first full year under the new strategy. They were intended to document progress, by the numbers, with an eye toward the evolving improvement. The first hundred days were all about turning the company around so that it could face a future in which earning the right to grow was feasible and really would result in growth.

But our focus in this chapter has been the first hundred days. The relevant question, therefore, is *Just what will we have after those days?*

Plenty.

There will be a complete strategy and process for *earning the right to grow.* That is, we will be positioned for the turnaround, with our first best vision of what is critical to growth versus what is trivial and undeserving of our attention. This knowledge is the key that unlocks true strategic—that is, profitable—growth.

"I'm confident we'll achieve our goal by following this four-step system," I wrote in my letter to the company. "We will create something extraordinary here, and I ask that you join me for the ride."

And I really meant it.

Over and over again, I have seen entire companies pivot from panic and despair to productive confidence the moment they understand that the right to grow not only must be earned but that *they* are quite capable of earning it. With this realization comes a willing acceptance of responsibility and accountability for transforming their company. It is quite a drama to behold, and it is even better when *you* are making it happen.

Town Hall

The town hall was meant to encourage people to speak candidly, but it was not a free-for-all. It had a very basic structure. It was a two-hour meeting, with the first sixty minutes devoted to my delivering a status report—an assessment of where Rolling Thunder stood at the moment. This assessment was based on my walking around the company and talking with people and, of course, also on the core meeting I had held with the ELT. In addition to the report, the team and I came to the town hall with that other key deliverable: a statement of the company's new goal to be attained within the span of the five-year plan.

So, within the first half of the town hall, I stated the goal. In doing so, I leveled with my audience, using an approach built on the Stockdale paradox. I'll explain this in just a little bit, but all you need to know at this point is that it is a way of delivering the unvarnished truth, the bad, the ugly, and the good—because there is always good—and to do so without fostering unwarranted and unthinking rose-colored optimism yet also without deepening panic and killing morale. I avoid the first pitfall—unfounded optimism—by keeping the varnish off the truth. I avoid the second—despair—by telling those in the town hall exactly what *I* am going to do, what *they* are going to do, and, most important of all, what *we* are going to do together. At this point, I keep it simple but meaningful. *Our immediate objective*, I say, *is to turn the company around so that we can earn the right to grow.*

Having ended the first hour with a frank assessment of the current situation and a basic statement of what we are going to do to win, we go into the second hour. The next sixty minutes of the town hall are devoted to answering questions from the participants. I know that there will be more questions than answers. As CEO, I need more answers. I need the answers to the team's questions, answers based on the data emanating from the organization. That means I need to ask the right questions and then listen to as many answers as I can get.

Sounds good. But time is my enemy, and I need to do everything I can to accelerate my learning. So, I go about the questioning more formally. In advance of the town hall, I draw up a questionnaire and ask employees to answer as many questions as they can. I make sure that they turn in their answers before the town hall, so that I can read them. I choose certain questions to bring up and discuss in the town hall. Time permitting, I open the proceedings to some spontaneous questions.

Accelerate Your Learning with a Questionnaire

Questions to Ask About the Past
Performance

How did the company perform in the past?

How do people in the organization think it performed?

How were goals set?

Were goals realistic?

Were goals insufficiently or overly ambitious?

Were internal or external benchmarks used?

What evaluative measures were employed?

What behaviors did they encourage and discourage?

What were the consequences if goals were not met?

Root Causes

If past performance was good, why? If poor, why?

How did the company's strategy, structure, technical capabilities, culture, and politics affect performance?

History of Change

What efforts have been made to change the company and what were the results?

Who was most instrumental in shaping this organization?

Questions to Ask About the Present
Strategy

What is the stated vision/strategy of the company?

Is the company genuinely pursuing the stated vision/strategy? If no, why? If yes, is the strategy likely to take the organization where it needs to go?

People

Who is capable and who is not?

(continued)

(*continued*)

Who is trustworthy and who is not?

Who are the influencers and why?

Processes

What are the key processes of the organization?

Are they effective? If not, why not?

Dangers

What dangers lurk? What are the risks?

Early Wins

Where can you achieve some early wins?

Questions About the Future

Challenges and Opportunities

What areas pose the greatest challenges next year? (Can anything be done now to prepare for them?)

What are the most promising unexploited opportunities? (How can they be realized?)

Barriers and Resources

What are the highest barriers to needed change?

What high-quality resources can be leveraged?

What new capabilities need to be developed or acquired?

Culture

What cultural changes need to be preserved or nurtured changed?

What cultural changes need to be changed?

What are the most promising unexploited growth opportunities?

Ask stakeholders: "If you were me, where would you focus your attention?"

When I feel that I have seen, heard, and, most of all, learned enough about the company, only then do I *really* start talking. I'll bet you that somewhere sometime somebody told you the so-called secret of giving a good speech: *Tell them what you are going to tell them, tell them, tell them what you've just told them.* Well, I'm here to tell you, as advice goes, this is pure, unadulterated gold.

In fact, I had already delivered the first part of the secret formula in the letter I circulated before the town hall and the second part during the first few minutes of the town hall. Now, I focused on the third part. I began by giving an orderly shape to the task we faced together: "I'd like to share a bit about where we are now, where we're going, and how we'll get there." It's simple. The people in front of me knew the company was in trouble. They felt lost, as in directionless. So, my job was to give them direction:

1. We are *here*. (In trouble.)

2. We are going *there*. (To a brighter, better future.)

3. Let me show you the way. (I am the truth and the life—okay, okay, the gospel might be a bridge too far.)

If you feel you are lost, you want directions. You don't want to be scolded, and you don't want to be called a bad name. I never wagged my finger at anyone, and I certainly did not get personal. But I did tell the truth as I saw it, by the numbers. We are *here*—and we don't want to be here. If what I said in this part of the town hall sounds like repetition, that's because it most certainly was:

> *"Today, Rolling Thunder is missing sales targets, and our costs are increasing."*

I didn't say much more than this before moving on to what immediate actions we were going to take to get out of *here* and start moving toward *there*:

> "*We must take immediate action to remedy this to steady the company.*"

Please note the pronoun. It is *we*, not *I, me, they, them, or you*. It is *we, we, we, we* all the way home.

I'm betting you've seen—and maybe more than once—the 1992 Tom Cruise, Demi Moore, Jack Nicholson movie *A Few Good Men*. If not, I'll leave you the unspoiled pleasure of watching the film for yourself. But everyone who's seen it can quote the exchange between Nicholson (playing USMC Colonel Nathan Jessup in command of the Marine platoon stationed at Guantanamo Bay, Cuba) and Cruise (playing Navy Lieutenant Daniel Kaffee, a JAG lawyer defending two marines accused of murder). Cruise is questioning Jessup, goading him into revealing that his order of an illegal Code Red caused the death of the marine Kaffee's clients are accused of killing.

Kaffee asks Jessup if he ordered the Code Red. The judge, seeking to protect Jessup's Fifth Amendment right not to incriminate himself, interjects that he does not have to answer. The arrogant colonel snaps back that he *will* answer. Kaffee taunts the colonel by demanding "the truth." Colonel Jessup roars in response that Kaffee "can't handle" the truth. Turns out Kaffee can handle it—and so can the people working in a company in need of a turnaround to a direction leading toward earning the right to grow. When you face them, it will be hard *not* to feel that they can't handle the truth. But if you guide them to the truth and deal with that truth together, you will discover that not only can they handle it, they desperately want and need to handle it. The secret here is that even in a hard situation, a scary situation, the truth, painful as it might be, has power, maybe just enough power to propel the group forward and upward.

This is the magic of the Stockdale paradox I mentioned previously. It is a lesson learned and shared by the late Admiral Jim Stockdale, highest-ranking US military officer to be held as a POW during the Vietnam War. He was imprisoned under horrific conditions from 1965 to 1973. Years later, Jim Collins, the author of *Good to Great*, talked to him, asking him how he got through it unbroken.

"I never doubted not only that I would get out," Stockdale explained, "but also that I would prevail in the end and turn the experience into the defining event of my life, which, in retrospect, I would not trade."

Collins was too awestruck to express any disbelief. Instead, he followed up by asking, "Who *didn't* make it out?"

"Oh, that's easy," Stockdale answered. "The optimists."

When Collins looked puzzled, the admiral elaborated. He explained that the optimists "were the ones who said, 'We're going to be out by Christmas.' And Christmas would come, and Christmas would go. Then they'd say, 'We're going to be out by Easter.' And Easter would come, and Easter would go. And then Thanksgiving, and then it would be Christmas again. And they died of a broken heart."

Stockdale told Collins that this taught him that while you must never lose your confidence that you will ultimately prevail, you cannot let that belief make you complacent and reliant on things over which you have no control. You cannot let wishful optimistic thinking cause you to abandon the "discipline to confront the most brutal facts of your current reality, whatever they might be."

Today, this approach has a name. It's called the Stockdale paradox, and it is about how knowing the truth, even the most dismal truth, helps you maintain the discipline to find your way through the worst problems. What you need is a *process* and the discipline to follow that process. Process can mean the difference between rational hope and panic-stricken despair.

Panic and despair are the products of inaction, a sense of not knowing what to do, a feeling of being unable to do anything, certainly anything capable of *turning it around*. So, when I walk into a troubled company, I aim to give the people something to do. I provide a direction. As is often the case when I am called in, the first thing or first few things that need doing are starkly obvious. The boat is leaking, so you plug the holes. The house is burning, so you put out the fire. I wrote in my letter to the people of Rolling Thunder: "We will quickly cut spending and initiatives not tied to revenue generation to provide a laser focus on the most important priorities for our success."

After this, I looked to the future and invited my audience to look with me. That's especially important because, right now, these poor folks were far from certain that they had any future—at least not with Rolling Thunder. The wisdom behind this approach is so old it's biblical: "Where there is no vision, the people perish." I did not promise anyone that they would surely succeed—no sweat. But I did promise them a vision: "Over the next few days, weeks and months, we'll implement many changes to secure this company's health."

Even by itself, promising that "we'll implement many changes" is important because the one thing most people in a distressed organization clearly understand is that they need change. If they give it even a little thought, they also understand—without anyone having to tell them—that to make tomorrow different from today, they have to do something different today. However, promising change, while *necessary* to turning a company around, is not *sufficient* to do so. Therefore, I laid out a process: "These changes," I wrote, "will be tied to my four-step system, which takes three to four months to complete."

33

Panic

Give Them a System

Ponder my sentence for just a moment. I linked the promised changes to *my four-step system*. In truth, the system is hardly unique to me, but I claimed ownership of it because I have used it successfully, I continue to use it, and I propose to use it some more. The *my* is not a patent claim, and, believe it or not, it is not an exercise in ego gratification. It is a promise that I understand the system, have expertise in implementing the system, and accept personal accountability for the system. This means that the people of this company, who will be using my system, are not only getting directions from the horse's mouth but are being pulled by the horse himself.

As for the word *system*, it is far better than *plan*. *System* is a set of principles and procedures that tell everyone how to do something. A *system* is a well-organized framework, a tested method. A plan, by contrast, expresses an aspiration, a hope, an intention. Modify the word *system* with *four-step* and you endow that system with a lot of exactitude. It is *four* steps, not *two*, not *five*, and certainly not *several* or a *bunch of*. The specificity gives my solution instant credibility. Even more impactful is framing the system in terms of time: a hundred days. It is an accurate, truthful estimate of how long the initial phase of the turnaround will take. This is fortunate because if you and your organization are standing on what many business writers like to call a "burning platform," you don't have the luxury of time. The downside of a burning platform is obvious: the business goes up in smoke and you with it. The upside, however, is also quite significant: standing on a burning platform is highly motivating. People in this situation *want* to make needed change happen, especially if they will see the results in just 90 to 120 days.

As a phrase, "the first hundred days" has a magical ring to it. Ever since the days of President Franklin D. Roosevelt, Americans have judged the performance of new occupants of the White House by what they accomplish or fail to accomplish in their first hundred days. To be sure, FDR set the bar remarkably high. He began his first term in 1933 by summoning Congress into a three-month special session during which he presented and gained passage of fifteen major bills enacting programs specifically aimed at combating the devastating effects of the Great Depression. Urged on by the president, Congress passed a grand total of seventy-seven laws in a hundred days. That's 0.77 laws per day, for those who want to keep score. America—indeed, the world—was a "burning platform" in 1933, and change was demanded.

FDR's first hundred days were jam-packed with substance. No wonder the president and his supporters were quick to brand those first three months as *the hundred days*. It was a phrase with a powerful Napoleonic ring, because it had long been used to describe the remarkable period bounded by the French emperor's bold return to France from his first exile (to Elba) on February 26, 1815, and his final defeat at Waterloo on June 18 of that same year. Between these events, Napoleon singlehandedly rebuilt an army of 250,000 and very nearly succeeded in retaking his lost empire. To this very day, no span of time carries greater symbolic weight than a hundred days. Like Napoleon and Roosevelt, I made shameless use of it. Well, leaders who have existential problems staring them in the eye need all the help they can get.

All four steps that I presented in the letter discussed previously in this chapter were to be completed within a hundred days. This did not mean that we would have a final and finished road to triumph. As I wrote in summarizing Step 4, "We won't wait for perfection here. We'll make sound, informed decisions and go." That is, once we had completed Step 4, we would have a rough-draft action plan put together. At that point, the managers throughout the company and the executive leadership team would bifurcate their efforts. Most of the managers would focus on drawing up action plans for

35

Panic

executing the "critical few" objectives, which directly addressed the 20 percent of customers and 20 percent of products that produce 80 percent of the company's revenue. In parallel with this, the C-suite executives would continue to develop a more complete strategy. This strategic management process would take about a year and would be the primary vehicle on which the company would ride to its five-year goal.

The Hundred-Day Job Interview

Whatever else the first hundred days are, consider them an extended job interview. As CEO, you own the goal that was set for the three- or five-year plan. You own the goal, but the organization's executive and operational leaders need to own the vehicles by which that goal will be reached: the strategy and its execution. This means that these leaders must be 100 percent on board with the goal and committed to the strategy as laid out in the first hundred days. As CEO, your job is to monitor and assess that commitment. By the third meeting of the four that span the first hundred days, it should become obvious who is on board and who is not. If at any point any team member's commitment seems doubtful to you, intervene. If, by the end of the third town hall meeting, the dubious party is not on board, you must conclude that they are not suited to the mission, which is to attain the goal that has been set. The remedy? Replace that person. Fail to take this step, and you greatly reduce the likelihood that *you* will fulfill *your* mission, which is to attain the goal you have set and for which you are accountable.

Now, the first hundred days does not run on automatic pilot. The town hall that launches it is only the first of three town halls.

We meet at the end of each month of the hundred-day period to discuss and measure our progress, to monitor our course, and to make any necessary corrections. As with the first town hall, half the next two meetings is devoted to questions and answers. The third meeting corresponds to the end of the quarter. Even after the first hundred days, we continue to convene town halls at the conclusion of each quarter.

Q1 Results

The third town hall meeting of the first hundred days is accompanied by a financial review that essentially summarizes the effect of those days. The review covers three general topics:

1. Summary and situational assessment
2. Approaches and actions
3. Financial headlines

The objective is to be honest and unflinching. Typically, the first review will show little or no improvement over what the situation was like at the beginning of the hundred days. In the case of Rolling Thunder:

- Declining financial results
- Significant level of projects and initiatives under way absent return on investment considerations and situational awareness of cash flow
- Concerns about the team
- Financial data, analytics, and KPI/tracking capabilities severely lacking
- Add-back limitations, cash situation, severance, and contractual cash requirements restrain nearest term levers

---

Panic

People need to know that there are no miracles to be had. But one thing is obvious. The people of Rolling Thunder now know where they stand. And if they stand in the basement, well, at least you can't fall out of a basement. So, much of this end-of-quarter town hall was devoted to approaches and actions to earning the right to grow. In the case of Rolling Thunder, earning the right to grow—turning the company around—required four immediate actions:

1. Align the organization on the current state to establish urgency of action.
2. Reaffirm the goal.
3. Establish an initial organization for strategy development.
4. Launch *now* whatever improvement actions can be launched *now*.

Chapter 2

Replace Uncertainty with Insight

Today's knowledge workers waste a third of their day, every day, on activities that could be reduced, consolidated, or eliminated altogether.
—William Heitman, *The Knowledge Work Factory*, 2019

Fear is a part of business. It is both an inevitable and an important part because business is all about evaluating and balancing risk and reward, the basic assumption being that there is never reward without risk. Like any other factor or force in business, fear must be managed. Admittedly, there is a lot that makes managing fear highly challenging. For one thing, it is hardwired into every animal, people included. If it weren't, few of us would stay alive for very long. So, there's that. But hardwired or not, some people scare easily while others don't scare easily enough. The essential tool for regulating fear—for knowing when to heed your fears and knowing when not to take counsel of your fears—is knowledge, experience-based know-how driven by abundant, timely, and accurate data.

The Dangerous Call to Action

With good reason, we tend to believe that complacency is the deadliest danger a business faces. An instinctive embrace of the status quo is toxic, make no mistake, but it is less a cause of certain death than another imperative that drives many businesses and the decisions their leaders make. It is this go-to knee-jerk command: *Don't just sit there. Do something!* Reflexes are reactive. Physiologists speak of a "reflex arc," a neuromuscular route from stimulus to response that bypasses all the higher thought centers of the brain. Some reflexes are life-saving, but they are always reactive, and if mere reaction is allowed to drive a business, it will, sooner or later, drive it right into a ditch.

Look, there is a lot to be said for cultivating a general bias for action. But the reflexive pressure to do something—*anything*—is, like all nonstrategic actions, liable to be futile at best and more immediately destructive at worst. This does not mean that the correct response either to an opportunity or a problem is to pull the covers over your head and go back to sleep. What it does mean is that it is almost always better not merely to just *stand* there, but to sit down and take time to understand the current situation, the business involved in that situation, and the broader business, political, market, technological, and other relevant contexts of the current situation.

Understanding is not only key to knowing what to do and how and when to do it, but to fill the void of ignorance. In the absence of data, knowledge, and understanding there is an intellectual and emotional vacuum almost instantly filled by FUD: fear, uncertainty, and doubt. FUD is insidious because it masquerades as the thoughtfulness of prudent caution. In fact, it is neither more nor less than the absence of knowledge and insight. It *feels* like something real because it produces acute discomfort. But it is a void that needs to be filled with data.

In the context of business, fear often takes a powerful hold because the pressure to do something is almost always backed by a not-so-thinly-veiled threat. Even experienced leaders are always aware of being judged by their performance, and when the job involves exploiting a narrow window of opportunity or guiding a critical turnaround, such judgment comes quickly, harshly, and often unconditionally.

From Panic to Profit

Uncertainty is partly a function of not immediately knowing what to do, but it is further compounded by imagination. In the absence of knowledge, imagination paints vivid images of the consequences of failure. The most effective first aid against the emotional ravages of uncertainty is to admit that of course you don't know what to do because you do not yet understand—or fully understand—the current unfolding situation. This is true of any new situation. It is not a disparagement of your competence or ability. Fortunately, the very fact that you don't understand because you don't yet know enough tells you and tells you clearly what to do. You must take immediate steps to get the data you need to build the knowledge and the insight you need. Once you have this information in hand, you will be positioned to decide what to do next.

FUD is by no means a good thing, but it is a powerful motivator. Unfortunately, it motivates nonstrategic actions. Although it is true that a shot in the dark sometimes finds its target, a miss is more likely. Worse, you might hit an innocent bystander. FUD drives decisions ranging from suboptimal to catastrophic. Clearly, you need to find an alternative form of motivation. You need the opposite of FUD, which is clarity. Clarity does not require genius, but it does require data and data analysis, which means gathering information and thinking about it. The reward for this effort is a shot at making strategic decisions that prompt actions capable of earning your organization the right to profitable growth.

Why It Is Better to Create Truth Rather Than Find It

We always talk about "finding" the truth. As the UFO/ET-hunting Special Agent Fox William Mulder liked to say on *The X-Files*, "The truth is out there." This implies that it is up to us to find it out there. Indeed, we would be suspicious of anyone who might say, "We need to create the truth," rather than, "We need to find the truth." Yet the truth about the truth is that it is *found* through clarity, and clarity is something we *create*.

We create clarity by actively seeking, actively looking, actively seeing, and actively thinking about what we see. We question what we believe we see. We strive to gain a clearer picture in a greater context. We work hard to remove the distractions and the mirages from our field of vision. Seeing clearly is essential, but thinking is also required. When we *create* clarity, rejecting all the smoke and dust and muck of FUD that gets in the way, we have an excellent chance of *finding* the truth. Armed with the truth, we have something useful for executing strategic growth.

But how do you create clarity—and not just create it, but create it quickly?

Recall what General Patton did when he first arrived in North Africa to take command of the defeated and demoralized US II Corps. He looked. The sight he *found* before his eyes was a mob of discouraged and undisciplined men. What he *created* from this sight was the *clarity* that translated what he saw into what it signified, namely, that a mob is not an army. To win a war, you need an army, not a mob. This clarity, which he *created*, enabled him to find the truth. The truth was that he had to furnish the leadership necessary to turn a mob into an army. Having found the truth, he knew what he had to do: introduce discipline. Without discipline a mob can never become an army. The beauty of this chain of reasoning, which replaced FUD with clarity, is that it did not take long to achieve.

No doubt, thinking was required. Patton had to figure out the best way to introduce discipline fast. As we saw, he began by strictly enforcing—to the letter—all Army regulations governing uniforms, including wearing properly knotted neckties, carefully laced leggings, and very uncomfortable helmets. Each of these items reminded the men who wore them that they were not an unruly mob but an army.

What is more, they were *Patton's* army, which gave them a special commitment to victory.

Neckties, leggings, and helmets did not magically create the army Patton and the nation needed, but these things were the first steps in a process that did create that much-needed army, transforming a defeated military unit into the consistently victorious II Corps. If, as a leader, you know what to do first, you are well on your way to knowing what to do next. You have the beginning of a *process*, which is productive action toward a strategic goal.

When I became CEO of Rolling Thunder, an organization with great yet unrealized potential, I resisted the urge to see a mob I could blame for flailing. The blaming urge results from viewing the world through the cracked and filthy lenses of FUD. One thing I didn't need was more FUD. So, I created clarity. I decided that I was not seeing the failure of a team but a problem of leadership and management. Having created this degree of clarity, I set about finding the truth of the situation. I walked around. I observed. I asked employees and managers questions. I listened to their answers.

Before I laid out to Rolling Thunder's management team the process discussed in Chapter 1, I did what strategically motivated executives do. I took a leaf from the book of physics. The goal of physicists is to understand how the universe behaves. They go about this by making careful observations and measurements, of course, but the real key is that they express what they observe and measure using numbers. If you get the numbers, you can do the math. In physics, the math translates the behavior of the universe into numbers, variables, and equations. These are faster to experiment with—to examine from all sides—than big planets, subatomic particles, and energy fields of all kinds. That's why physicists express the behavior of nature in numbers. Business leaders, when tasked with turning a company around so that it can earn the right to grow, likewise express the behavior of the company in numbers. These numbers are not hard to find. Every business generates them. It is the task of the executive to engage with this data.

But how?

Over the long history of their science, physicists have formulated a variety of natural laws that help them make sense of the data all physical phenomena produce. We who manage businesses are fortunate to have an extraordinarily valuable natural law ready-made, which is also a social, economic, and commercial law. It is the Pareto principle.

The Blessing of Uneven Distribution

Vilfredo Federico Damaso Pareto was born on July 15, 1848, in Paris. His family were Genoese nobility, but like many enlightened Europeans in the 1840s, they held revolutionary values. They fled to Paris to escape royal authorities in Italy and, when their son was born, Mom and Dad gave him a German name, Wilfried Fritz, in honor of the German Revolution of 1848. They didn't change it to the more Italian Vilfredo Federico until they moved back to Italy in 1858.

The young Vilfredo demonstrated his genius early on. He was admitted to the most advanced schools, including the newly opened Instituto Technico Leardi. From here, he went on to the Polytechnic University of Turin (at the time called the Technical School for Engineers) and earned a doctorate in engineering. The title of his doctoral dissertation, "The Fundamental Principles of Equilibrium in Solid Bodies," sounds both highly specialized and super nerdy. But Pareto believed he was onto something big, and he devoted much of his professional life to defining principles of equilibrium and, even more important, disequilibrium, not just as these principles applied to solid bodies but to sociology, economics, and commerce as well. He found disequilibrium everywhere, and he believed that much could be accomplished if he could understand this disequilibrium phenomenon better.

Pareto was a certified polymath who refused to confine his intelligence to this or that pigeonhole. He worked as a highly paid engineer in a variety of industries until, in his mid-forties, he took everything he had learned as an engineer and poured it into economics and business management, which he taught at the University of Florence before moving on to become chairman of the Political Economy Department at the University of Lausanne in Switzerland.

Through a jam-packed and varied career, Pareto somehow found time to pursue his favorite leisure-time passion, gardening. He had a special fondness for pea plants. Even while getting his hands dirty, however, he never shut down the analytical side of his brain. As he tended his garden, he could not stop calculating. His calculations revealed that roughly 20 percent of the pea plants in his garden produced roughly 80 percent of his viable peapods. This insight stuck in his craw, and he carried it with him out to the world beyond his garden. He discovered that the 80/20 ratio was not peculiar to peas but was pretty much characteristic of the whole universe, whether natural or human made. He saw that what he dubbed "uneven distribution" applied almost everywhere he looked—from pea plants to the distribution of wealth among the people of Italy. Concerning that, he calculated that 80 percent of the nation's land was owned by just 20 percent of the nation's population. He turned to industrial production and demonstrated that 80 percent of industrial output came from just 20 percent of industrial companies. Before long, he applied the 80/20 rule to just about every system or process whose input and output could be quantified, which, come to think about it, is pretty much everything.

So . . . What?

Today, people call what Pareto discovered the Pareto principle, the 80/20 rule, or even the law of the critical few and the trivial many.

Replace Uncertainty with Insight

It holds sway as something very close to a natural law, this truth that a minority of actions, causes, and inputs produces the majority of results, outputs, and rewards. It holds true, at least roughly, in anything, everywhere. But how does knowing this 80/20 thing help *my* business?

"Know thyself" was a good enough idea to have been chiseled into the pediment of the Temple of Apollo at Delphi. So, begin by turning 80/20 on yourself, on what you do, and on how you work. To the extent that you can quantify your activity, you will find that roughly 80 percent of what you accomplish in, for instance, your job comes from just 20 percent of the time you spend working at it. To express this even more discouragingly, 80 percent of what you do is trivial.

If this makes you feel bad, don't take it too personally. William Heitman, author of *The Knowledge Work Factory*, points out that knowledge workers waste a third of their day "on activities that could be reduced, consolidated, or eliminated altogether." Harsh as this sounds, the Pareto principle tells us that this estimate is actually way too generous. The waste is closer to two-thirds. But it's not just you. It's all of us.

Do you remember what happened when the black-shrouded figure of the Ghost of Christmas Yet to Come showed Ebenezer Scrooge a vision of his own unmourned death and the very profoundly mourned death of sweet, innocent Tiny Tim?

Well, I'll remind you. Scrooge asked the ghost to answer one question. "Are these the shadows of the things that *will* be, or are they shadows of things that *might* be, only? . . . Assure me that I yet may change these shadows you have shown me by an altered life!"

And you know the rest. Even if you haven't read Dickens's *A Christmas Carol*, you surely have not escaped at least one movie or TV version of it. So, we all know that Ebenezer Scrooge awakens from his Christmas Eve nightmares a changed man. He has now seen the data revealing what his cold, unfeeling, miserly, selfish life has produced and has failed to produce. He thinks about what he saw and is rewarded with insight. He resolves that he will no longer waste his life on the selfish and uncharitable things that produce no happiness and no good. He will instead choose to invest what remains of his life in matters that enhance love, nurture humanity, and generate happiness.

If you look on today and find it unsatisfactory, you will surely hope that tomorrow will be different. But why settle for hope? If you want tomorrow to be different from today, do something different today! That is the lesson Scrooge learns, and it is a lesson made many times more effective by 80/20.

If roughly 80 percent of what you do produces nothing but trivial results, why not stop doing that 80 percent and focus instead on the 20 percent of what you do that produces critical results? Use the 80/20 insight to alter what you do with your precious time and effort so that the trivial gloom makes way for a bright future. And bear in mind, this uneven distribution applies to your efforts, to work generally, and to markets, customers, products—every aspect of business. Don't be discouraged, and don't be intimidated. Instead, take hold of 80/20 as you would any other tool of your trade. Make use of this natural law to understand your business and then to optimize its performance. You are not a helpless, hapless bystander. Take strategic action to turn the uneven distribution of input and output to your advantage. The Pareto principle points you and your business toward a competitive edge.

Measure Only to Improve

Business has been awash in reports for longer than most of us have been in business or even alive. I was amused to discover that one Erwin Knoll, a *Washington Post* journalist who became the editor of *The Progressive,* a left-leaning journal founded by Senator Robert M. LaFollette Sr. in 1909, noted in the 1960s that New York City's

Department of Mental Hygiene "produced and distributed a three-page illustrated memorandum on how to split an English muffin."

I bet there were loads of measurements in that memorandum. Reports have a lot of measurements. These can be useful, and, in fact, a good report starts with the key measurements. These are the basic data required to understand most things, especially in business. The problem with a great many reports, however, is that they fail to get beyond the measurements. To be useful, a report must begin with the data—the objective measurements—but must then conclude by applying those measurements (the data) to *improvement*. In fact, I'm not going to condemn a muffin memo I haven't read for myself. For all I know, it concludes by telling you how to split a muffin to perfectly optimize its flavor. If that's the case, the muffin memo deserves to stand as one of the great memos in history, and I hope somebody finds it and republishes it. My point is that if most reports had as their objective transforming data into improvement, very few people would complain about being buried under too many reports. In fact, the majority would clamor for more.

This is why I love the 80/20 principle and want everyone to share my love for it. 80/20 is all about turning data into improvement. So, I'm going to repeat my simple rule for ensuring continuous improvement: *If you want tomorrow to be different from today, do something different today*. The question is, what should that something be? The answer is found by applying 80/20. It shows you precisely what to do different.

Apply 80/20 to employees, customers, markets, products, and processes to improve how the business handles all of them to achieve strategic growth, which is (if the strategy is worthwhile) profitable growth. If you are wasting resources today and don't want to waste them tomorrow, stop wasting them today. Your first step is to identify the critical and devote your resources to these opportunities instead of to the trivial. Instead of doing what Vilfredo Pareto observed that we usually do—namely, input 80 percent of whatever we have in order to get a measly 20 percent gain—we can decide to stop diverting resources from what is critical to what is trivial. To put it another way, just as Scrooge chose not to be the victim of the terrifying Ghost of Christmas Yet to Come but instead asked him if change is possible, so we can decide to stop being bullied by the Pareto principle and instead use it to improve performance.

Segment Is a Verb

By all means, let's measure. But let's measure what must be measured to create improvement. You need to *segment*—sort and separate wheat from chaff—your customers and your products to ensure that your business devotes as much as 80 percent of its resources to the products and customers that are most productive.

First, gather the necessary data:

1. For each product, record total sales, number of customers who purchased the product, and gross margin.

2. For each customer, record total sales.

Gross margin (GM) is a universally respected indicator of financial performance. It is the difference between revenue and cost of goods sold (COGS), divided by revenue:

$$GM = (Revenue - COGS) / Revenue$$

This formula will yield a percentage, which is the conventional expression of gross margin. Calculate the GM for each product.

Replace Uncertainty with Insight

Second, analyze the data:

1. List the products in descending order of their total sales, that is, from highest to lowest.
2. List the customers in descending order by total sales, that is, from most dollars to least.

Third, segment the products and customers by identifying the top 20 percent of each. That is, draw a line between 20 and 21 percent. The products and customers above the line are, by absolute definition, the critical few. The rest, also by definition, are the trivial many.

Like many words in the English language, *segment* can be used as a noun or a verb. When you are working to earn the right to grow, to turn the business around, you need to use it as a verb. If action is demanded of leadership, take the most effective action you can: take a step toward strategic growth by segmenting your business, revealing the company's critical few products and customers, the ones that will earn you the right to grow.

X Marks the Spot

You've taken a big step in the right direction. You now know something about the critical few versus the trivial many. But what *this* segmentation does not tell you is how the product data intersects with the customer data. Your objective is to make the uneven distribution of the Pareto principle work for you. Right now, roughly 80 percent of your resources are dedicated to producing just 20 percent of your GM. To earn the right to grow, you need to do better. You need to harness the uneven distribution as an engine of growth by more efficiently deploying your resources chiefly to serve both high-performing products and high-performing customers. To do this, you need a way to find the intersection of product data and customer data. This is the critical intersection.

Looking only at products provides a partial and even distorted picture of what your key customers, call them your A customers, are buying from you. Customers typically purchase an array of products, many related to one another. Earning the right to grow demands understanding more than the cumulative sales of products. It requires developing a picture of your customers' needs and wants as they are made manifest in the complete basket of products they buy from you.

By the same token, looking only at your customers will cause you to miss why different customers end up in different quadrants. When you have a picture of the *intersection* of products and customers, you can see basic patterns in customer behavior that will guide the strategic design of your systems and processes. There is a reason why in cartoon depictions of treasure maps x always marks the spot. It is an intersection. In selling goods to customers, the intersection of products and customers is the x marking the spot directly under which your treasure lies. Anyone who has read Robert Louis Stevenson knows that finding buried treasure requires having a treasure map. The map in *Treasure Island* shows where you are and then draws a meandering line to where the treasure is, marked by that iconic x. Maps drawn using 80/20 data and analysis look very different from this. Yet they are still treasure maps, which lead not to one but to four intersections of customers and the products they buy. Only one of those intersections is critical. You really need this map.

Quads

Having gathered your data and segmented products and customers so that you have identified the best performers (the top 20 percent) among both, you can now take the segmentation process to the next operation, which is sorting your products and customers into a chart consisting of four quadrants or quads. See Figure 2-1 for a sample quad chart.

Replace Uncertainty with Insight

PRODUCTS

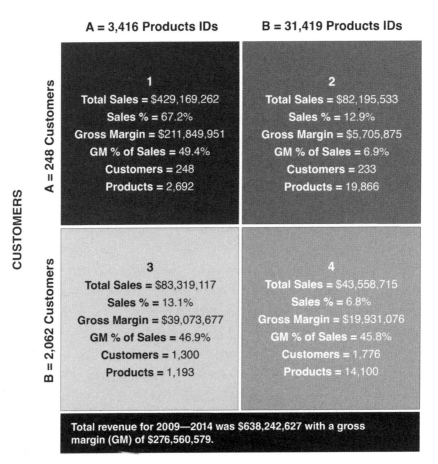

Figure 2-1 Sample 80/20 Quad Chart

The 80/20 rule tells us that 80 percent of output is produced by just 20 percent of input. That is, 80 percent of your sales are produced by just 20 percent of your customers (who are by definition your top-performing customers) buying 80 percent of your top-performing products (the top-performing products being just 20 percent of 100 percent of your products). Conversely, the remaining 80 percent of your customers produce just 20 percent of your sales. This being the case, 80/20 predicts the following:

Quad 1, A customers buying A products (0.8 × 0.8) = 64 percent of sales

Quad 2, A customers buying B products (0.8 × 0.2) = 16 percent of sales

Quad 3: B customers buying A products (0.2 × 0.8) = 16 percent of sales

Quad 4: B customers buying B products (0.2 × 0.2) = <u>4 percent of sales</u>

Total Sales = 100 percent

The reality reflected in the sample quad chart clearly varies from the 80/20 prediction:

Quad 1 sales: 67.2 percent (actual) versus 64 percent (predicted)

Quad 2 sales: 12.9 percent (actual) versus 16 percent (predicted)

Quad 3 sales: 13.1 percent (actual) versus 16 percent (predicted)

Quad 4 sales: 6.8 percent (actual) versus 4 percent (predicted)

Does the difference between actual sales and predicted sales give the lie to 80/20? No. Not at all.

The new-car window sticker that specifies miles per gallon (MPG)—or in the case of an electric vehicle, MPG equivalent—always cautions that "actual results will vary for many reasons." If you're like me, when your MPG performance fails to meet expectations, your first thought is that the manufacturer has somehow fudged the data. Doubtless, automakers (who are the ones responsible for running the MPG tests) take steps to ensure that the many factors that influence fuel performance are optimized. The car is tuned to optimum specs, the test driver operates at some optimum speed, does not lead-foot acceleration or slam on the brakes, and so on. But this is not fudging. It is operating the vehicle for the best fuel economy. We should all learn to trust MPG figures as reasonable theoretical targets, and provided that our aim as drivers is to achieve maximum fuel efficiency, we should try to change any driving habits that consume more fuel, whether fossil or electric. Those of us who cannot resist fast acceleration and hard braking will pay more for energy, and the delta between the *sticker* MPG and *our* MPG will widen.

As with actual versus predicted MPG, so with actual versus predicted 80/20 performance. Your mileage might vary for many reasons. Just don't blame Vilfredo Pareto. Instead, accept the predicted performance as quite possible, even feasible. The difference between the predicted performance and the actual performance is not due to an imperfection in the Pareto principle, but indicates the effect of forces, decisions, actions, and other factors in the business (and in the market and the economy) that are pushing or pulling the data out of sync with 80/20 expectation. Regard the gaps between the predicted and the actual performance not as indications of faults in the Pareto model but as meaningful deltas that warrant analysis and probably should prompt changes in such areas as strategy, tactics, policy, and personnel. Most immediately, the deltas should encourage different treatment for different levels of customer and product based on performance. Allocate more sales resources to your A customers and fewer resources to your B customers.

In the sample quad (Figure 2-1), note that the performance of A customers buying A products in Quad 1 exceeds the Pareto prediction by 3 percent. That's good! Right? But what does it mean for the business that just 248 customers (out of a total of 2,310) who buy just 2,692 products (out of a total of 31,419) are responsible for the high performance of Quad 1? At the same time, sales performance in Quads 2 and 3 is 3.1 and 2.9 percent (respectively) below the level the 80/20 Rule predicts. What product and resource allocation decisions should this motivate? Or look at Quad 4. It exceeds expectations by 2.8 percent. Perhaps more effort should be made to devote more resources to move some of these customers and products to a better quad. Perhaps demand justifies an increase in price. Or perhaps the overperformance of Quad 4 suggests that too many resources are being allocated to produce the extra 2.8 percent.

Bearing in mind the differences between predicted and actual performance as indicated in each quad, let's take a closer look at the nature of each of those four buckets. Quad 1 fits into the upper left of the chart. It consists of your A customers (the top 20 percent in terms of gross margin sales) and the A products (again, the top 20 percent in terms of gross margin sales) they buy. This quad is often labeled *the fort* because it generates roughly 80 percent of your sales and therefore demands to be protected, defended, served, and reinforced above the other three quads. Ideally, about 80 percent of your resources should be dedicated to serving Quad 1.

Quad 2 goes in the upper right corner of the chart and consists of your A customers and the B products (in terms of gross margin sales, distributed across the lower 80 percent) they buy. Quad 2 is sometimes dubbed the *necessary evil* because you are obliged to support it to satisfy those of your best customers who demand these products. True, the intersection of A customers and B products falls below the top 20 percent in gross margin productivity, but the resources you devote to this quad are nevertheless necessary because these B products keep a significant fraction of your A customers happy.

The bottom two quads consist of the B customers and the A and B products they buy. Quad 3, at the bottom left-hand corner of the quad chart, holds the B customers who buy A products. Even though, collectively, B customers make up the 80 percent of customers who ultimately produce just 20 percent of your sales, there is value here. Nevertheless, you need to take a measured approach to how much of your resources you put into selling this quadrant. The label *transactional* aptly describes Quad 3 because its value to the business is

55

Replace Uncertainty with Insight

realized only if its contents are offered and sold with minimal use of the company's resources. The objective is to offer the merchandise, take the orders, and ring up the sales. You would not devote your top 20 percent of sales personnel (yes, you can evaluate your sellers using 80/20) to servicing these sales in any time-consuming consultative manner. In fact, it would be best to handle these sales entirely online so that you can take the order, fulfill the order, and bank the money with minimal human intervention.

Finally, there is Quad 4. The best descriptive label for this quad is *price up or get out.* Here is where you collect the B customers who buy B products, your least profitable customers buying your least profitable products. There are differing approaches to this quad. Some authorities advocate categorically abandoning the customers and products who end up here. Doubtless, some do deserve to be dumped. Product/customer intersections that cost your business money are killing you. You don't want them. You literally cannot afford them. And remember: underperforming products and customers don't just cost you more than they earn for you—they bleed resources away from the top two quads. They aren't just a passive source of loss—they are an aggressive producer of loss, a drain on resources far better used elsewhere.

But that is the worst case for Quad 4. Always work the numbers. Thinking is required. Avoid the impulse to simply abandon Quad 4. Just take steps to ensure that selling here makes rather than loses money. Continue to offer those products you can price up to make a profitable sale. And bear in mind that raising the price is not the only means of making a product profitable. You can reduce HR headcount by making these products available only through online orders, for example. You can also impose minimum purchase requirements, and you can simplify your inventory by offering fewer models or colors of a given item. Whatever you cannot sufficiently price up or otherwise treat so that it turns a profit should be dropped from the inventory. If this means you also shed some B customers, so be it. (We will have much more to say about your strategic options later in the book.)

If all this sounds brutal, nothing is more brutal than working yourself, your employees, your other stakeholders, and your company itself to death. The 80/20 map identifies your treasure in the optimum intersection of products and customers so that you can efficiently serve this intersection and build profitable growth on it rather than fritter away some 80 percent of your resources on the trivial. *X* marks the spot.

I am not a preacher, but I do believe these words from the Sermon on the Mount have special value for executives and managers: "Where your treasure is, there will your heart be also." So, as far as your business is concerned, your heart should be in Quad 1, but serving and growing this treasure does not mean you can or should ignore the other quads. Quad 2 (A customers buying B products) must be served, albeit with less than your full heart. (It's cheaper that way.) Quad 3 (B customers buying A products) is to be served transactionally, using a minimum of resources. Quad 4 (B customers buying B products) contains at least some products and customers that not only are expendable but also must be dropped because they are toxic to your bottom line. If this alienates some customers in this quad, the hard fact is that your business is better off without them. They are costing you resources that should be allocated elsewhere. But even Quad 4 almost always has some value to offer. Products that can be sufficiently priced up to profitability or sold in ways that reduce costs and thereby cross the line into profitability should not be kicked out the door.

Replace Uncertainty with Insight

Obey Natural Law

The 80/20 quads are not magical—although, like other demonstrations of natural law, they might feel that way sometimes. In fact, quad analysis, which can be done entirely in a back office, a penthouse office, or at home in your basement, is not a full substitute for walking around your business and talking to managers and the folks on the shop floor. It does not take the place of talking to your sales force and talking to your customers. Day-to-day reality always has the last word.

No doubt, 80/20 quad analysis is a simplification of the real world, but it is a simplification that, done right, is far more helpful than distorting. Applying 80/20 is not the same as dumbing down reality. It is a way of avoiding gut-feeling seat-of-the-pants blind flying on the one hand and analysis paralysis on the other. All businesses are full of noise. 80/20 quad analysis cuts through the noise and lets you attune your ears to the signal. Yes, the 80/20 quads hide much of the nitty-gritty, the details of individual products and individual customers, but in so doing, they expose the contours of larger patterns. However imperfect, 80/20 analysis replaces FUD with sufficient clarity to at least begin a course of continuous improvement beyond suboptimal economics. 80/20 moves the organization in generally the right direction, and real-life, real-world vigilance will allow for course correction throughout the journey. Never let the perfect become the enemy of the good but always aim to elevate the good to the better and the better to the best. To earn the right to grow, don't look for a way out. Look for a way to your treasure.

Chapter 3

Transform Business Insights into Business Segments

Divide and rule.
—Machiavelli's favorite Latin maxim (*"Divide et impera"*)

The 80/20 ratio is real, and it's hardly the first time that mathematics has been used to understand the natural world. About 300 BCE, Euclid, the father of geometry, mentioned what was later called the *golden ratio* or even what the Italian Renaissance mathematician Luca Pacioli called it: *the divine proportion.* In strictly mathematical terms, the golden ratio is a ratio between two numbers that equals about 1.618. Sounds pretty random, but through the ages, this ratio has been regarded as an expression of beauty distilled to mathematics. In fact, like 80/20, it is a ratio found throughout nature. Leonardo da Vinci used it to illustrate the symmetry of everything from the shell of the nautilus to the proportions of the human body. The growth of pinecone seeds and many tree leaves present patterns that closely approximate the golden ratio. The same is true of sunflower spirals. The beauty of tree leaf growth is that the leaves on a given tree appear to proliferate in golden ratio patterns such that one leaf does not shade another, thereby promoting healthy growth. Artists, architects, and even engineers have harnessed the golden ratio to enhance the beauty, strength, and efficiency of their works (see Figure 3-1).

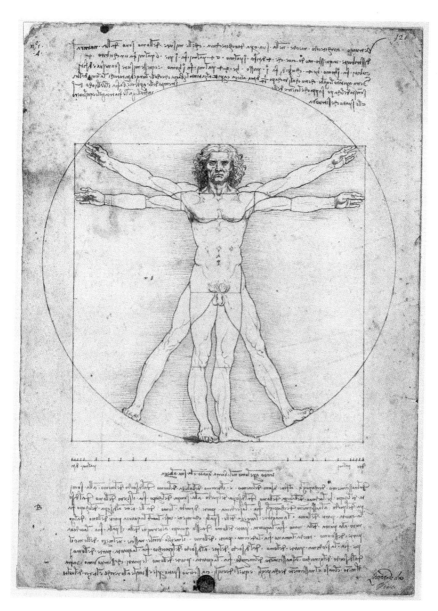

Figure 3-1 Leonardo da Vinci's "Vitruvian Man," an illustration of the Golden Ratio. (Collection, Gallerie dell'Accademia, Venice, CC 4.0).

Like the golden ratio, 80/20 appears to be nature's way of applying mathematics to the real world. If this seems magical or mystical—well, it is. After all, if you can't credit the universe for being awesome, what does it take to impress you? The truly awe-inspiring beauty of both the golden ratio and 80/20, however, is that they connect numbers—measurement, calculation, and analysis—directly to the real world, whether your interest is in observing the natural world, making a more beautiful work of art, or starting, running, continuously improving, and strategically growing a business.

Serving Simplification

80/20 is so powerful an instrument for understanding many aspects of the real world, business included, that there is a danger of losing sight of the realities to which it is applied. 80/20 can tell you a lot about your business, but it is more than a diagnostic instrument. It is a tool in service to simplification, which is a process for strategically focusing a business on what produces profitable growth rather than waste of investment.

80/20 guides you to simplifying your business. That does not mean making it easier or dumber. Even less does it mean firing a bunch of people or discarding a load of product lines willy-nilly. It is about identifying the products and customers who matter most to your business so that you can focus on over-resourcing them. 80/20 reveals that roughly 80 percent of your revenue comes from the intersection of 20 percent of your customers and 20 percent of your products. If, as proven by 80/20 analysis, 100 percent of your company's input (investment in products, personnel, and costs to acquire customers) yields just 20 percent of your gross revenue, then 80 percent of investment input is essentially wasted. Put another way, only 20 percent of your effort is critical to your success. The rest of what you do is expended on trivial activity, work that not only fails to build revenue but actually costs you money. It would be to your advantage to reallocate resources from that misspent 80 percent to overserve the critical 20 percent of your customers and products.

Simplification might require reducing the number of products or models in a product line, the number and range of customers your sales organization is focused on reaching, the number of employees required to make sales and to support customers, the complexity of processes involved in the business, and the geographical reach of the business. Most executives are quick to seize on opportunities to make personnel cuts and to find ways to streamline operations, but they often balk at the very idea of reducing product lines and, God forbid, shedding customers—no matter how unproductive many of those customers are.

The last-mentioned reluctance is understandable. After all, the great management guru Peter Drucker himself declared that the "purpose of business is to create and keep a customer," which is the opposite of lose a customer any day of the week. True, but that same Peter Drucker also concluded that companies tend to produce too many products in too great variety. He added that they also hire employees they don't need and expand into markets and economic sectors they would be far better off shunning. We can avoid putting mixed signals into Drucker's mouth by amending his declaration: *The purpose of business is to create and keep customers who produce profit while shedding those who produce only costs.* Add to this that *the purpose of business is to make and sell products that create and keep profitable customers while discontinuing those products that produce nothing but costs.*

How do we know which customers are which?

No need to guess. Just apply 80/20. In Chapter 2, we discussed how analyzing the data generated by your customers, products, sales, costs, profitability, markets, and regions can be used to segment your product/customer revenue into quads that reveal the performance of (1) your A products bought by A customers, (2) B products bought by A customers, (3) A products bought by B customers, and (4) your B products bought by B customers. Think of the quad as a treasure map that leads you to product/customer combinations generating roughly 80 percent of your gross revenue and significantly more than 80 percent of gross profits.

What do you do with this information?

To serve Quad 1, your A products/A customers (roughly the most productive 20 percent), you should allocate as near to 80 percent of your resources and effort as you can. Having done this, you can address the remaining three segments, Quads 2, 4, proportionally. Remember:

- Quad 1 is often called *the fort* and merits approximately 80 percent of the company's resources.

- Quad 2 is regarded as the *necessary evil* because the B products in this quadrant are bought by A customers, and you need to keep those customers happy. But you literally cannot afford to lavish the same degree of resources on Quad 2 as you devote to Quad 1. It's simple math. You can spend 80 percent of your assets on one or the other, but not both. Find a way to provide just the right level of resources to serve the combination in Quad 2 that will keep the A customers happy, even if that means minimal profit or break-even performance. Under no circumstances, however, should you allow this *necessary evil* to become a cost, a source of negative profit.

- Quad 3 products/customers consist of A products purchased by B customers. This segment is often labeled as *transactional*, meaning that it represents good business if you can run it on a strictly transactional basis, using the fewest possible resources (especially sales personnel). The profit here might not be strategic, but opportunistic profit is profit nonetheless. We'll discuss shortly some strategies for reducing the cost of sales in this segment.

- Quad 4 products/customers—essentially B products purchased by B customers—represents a small fraction of revenue, so that stocking and selling these underperforming products to these underperforming customers typically destroys margins. It is negative profit that costs your business. This segment is often labeled as *price up or out*. If you can turn a profit by raising prices and automating the selling process by shifting underperforming products to online orders only (we will look at some other strategies as well), keep selling. But don't bust your pick trying to salvage this combination of low-performing products and low-performing customers. Drop the products from your line. Won't this result in losing customers? You bet it will, but the customers you will lose are customers you cannot afford to keep.

Simplification Made Simple

The concept of *streamlining* is all about speed, right? Yes, but also no.

First and foremost, streamlining is about reducing drag, which is about reducing the waste of energy that could be used more productively to increase speed. If streamlining is *all* about anything, it is *all* about increasing efficiency by reducing entropy, the randomness that slows things down and makes work ("the transfer of energy by a force acting on an object as it is displaced") less efficient. A good example of the operation of entropy is found in the distressing fact that 80 percent of what you do is wasted on the trivial, leaving only 20 percent focused on the critical. Aircraft designers want as much of the thrust produced by the airplane's engines to be used for the critical work of providing lift and velocity. Anything that gets in the way of this needs to be streamlined—simplified, preferably simplified out of existence.

In designing and building your business, you want to increase efficiency and reduce drag by simplifying (reducing) product offerings and/or the number of models or variations of products offered. Sure, cutting back on the product line will likely result in the loss of some customers, but if you are careful to cut only the unprofitable products, the customers you lose are not the customers you need or even want. Serving any customer incurs costs. Serving a productive customer produces more revenue than cost. Serving an unproductive customer produces more cost than revenue. Who wants that? The unproductive customer is drag. Enough of it will pull your airplane right out of the sky.

Most of us in business have a natural urge to create customers and to want to keep them at any cost. There's a problem with that, because the cost of keeping customers at any cost is a nonstrategic cost far too high to bear. Paying it will kill the business, probably sooner rather than later. Apply 80/20 to bring your business back to strategic reality. And that reality does not necessarily mean running away from all B customers and B products. Price up what you can in Quad 4 until these B products selling to B customers turn a profit. The higher prices will almost certainly drive some of your lowest-end B customers away. So be it. Wish them well and say toodle-oo.

Quad 4 sales (of B products to B customers) should be made with minimum resource commitment from the sales force or support from anyone. This is also true, though less extreme, for Quad 3—A products purchased by B customers—but the A customers purchasing B products in Quad 2 expect some degree of sales force commitment and other support. They should receive it.

Can You Ever Be Too Simple?

It is possible to oversimplify. For example, if it is good to devise a strategy that devotes 80 percent of the company's resources to the 20 percent of customers who produce 80 percent of your gross revenue, why not devote 100 percent to them and just dump the lower 80 percent altogether? Another old saying that I've mentioned is to never let the best become the enemy of the good. It applies here. Start with the assumption that Quad 1—A customers buying A products—can't be simplified further than it already is because every customer and product here is productive. It just doesn't get any simpler than the happy situation presented in The Fort.

Next, turn to Quad 2, A customers buying B products. This segment is a bit more complex than the segment in Quad 1 because your B products are not as profitable as your A products. But some of them are still respectably profitable, and you have the added incentive that some of your best customers demand these products. So, despite the added complexity, you have two incentives to avoid overly aggressive simplification here. These are products that either make money or, at worst, break even. More important, at least some of your best customers, who are customers you really want to keep and therefore must satisfy, demand these products.

Even if the top two segments are pretty much off-limits to simplification, you are still left with a large number of products that are part of the group that produces just 20 percent of your gross revenue. All these are legitimate targets for simplification because they create unnecessary complexity that bleeds resources away from the A products. Many in Quad 4 can be jettisoned unless they can be made to generate profit. Those in Quad 3 have a better chance of being saved. This is where the dirty dozen comes in.

The Dirty Dozen

The *dirty dozen* is what I call my simplification toolbox of twelve tools to eliminate complexity from your organization. There's literally no better way to simplify than to get rid of stuff, and in this case it's your B products that offer no strategic advantage. If you price them high enough to turn a profit, nobody will buy them. If you lower the price, you can't clear your costs. You could give these products away and make no profit, or you could just scrub them out and get rid of them. No Scrubs is less a tool than a weapon, and sometimes only a weapon will do. As Al Capone put it, "You can get farther with a smile and a gun than you can with a smile." But the dirty dozen also has many other tools, kinder, gentler, and more nuanced, all dedicated to preventing the best from becoming the enemy of the good.

The first four dirty dozen tools relate directly to customers:

- **Can't Buy Me Love:** This tool cures leaders' obsession with getting and keeping customers at any cost by offering discounts. Instead, just stop offering discounts to B customers— especially B customers buying unprofitable B products. The greater the discount, the narrower the margin. Soon it vanishes altogether, and you lose money with each sale. Quads 3 and 4 cry out for pricing up or throwing out, not discounting.

- **Money for Nothing:** This tool is what you need to minimize the cost of selling to B customers. Stop paying sales commissions on most B-customer business.

- **Money (That's What I Want):** When you are in low-margin territory, you need a tool to simplify sales and fulfillment. For Quads 3 and 4, you could require payment by credit card up front—and then tack on a fee for good measure.

Transform Business Insights into Business Segments

- **All the Small Things:** Here is a tool to make an otherwise worthless sale worthwhile. Set a minimum-order value, quantity, or both on select B merchandise. In some situations, this treatment can be applied to entire lines of merchandise. Force the kind of sales that will make selling these items worth your while. There is no excuse for selling merchandise that cannibalizes your margins.

The next eight dirty dozen tools relate to products:

- **Circle of Life:** This tool calls for substituting A products from a preferred vendor for equivalent B products wherever possible. It pushes customers to buy from the A-product segments.

- **No Scrubs:** We've already met this tool. It empowers you to drop B products sold to B customers that have no strategic value. Don't throw good money after bad in an effort to rehabilitate what cannot be saved.

- **Ain't No Mountain High Enough:** This powerful tool must be used sparingly but when necessary. Before dropping a B product, you might try not just pricing it up but pricing it *way* up.

- **Take It or Leave It:** Offer your B products in a single standard package size and type with no customization. If customers want it, they must take it on your terms.

- **Time After Time:** Here's a tool that is not always thought of. Instead of filling orders on demand, piecemeal, aggregate them, holding fulfillment until you have enough orders in hand to create a margin. The customer can get this product, but it will take time.

- **Don't You (Forget About Me):** Specify scheduled days for service or order. Stop firefighting and scrambling for unprofitable business.

- **My Way:** Nineteenth-century Chicago retail tycoon Marshall Field ran his exclusive State Street department store under the banner of this mantra: *Give the lady what she wants.* That might have worked for Field, but it doesn't mean it will work for you. Here's a tool that gives *you* what *you* want. Limit availability of certain B products to a very few standard option packages. Ban mix-and-match options, which introduce a costly degree of complexity to the sale and increase your inventory overhead. You cannot afford to add unrecoverable costs to the merchandise. Sell it *your* way or not at all.

- **You've Got Another Thing Coming:** B products can sometimes be elevated to the high end of the B segment or even make the leap into A territory if you package them in sets. Instead of offering a specialized screwdriver that only a few customers need, make it available only in a set. To get this product, customers must buy the complete package. After the sale, they can always discard whatever they don't want. After all, it's a free country.

The 80/20 Miracle—Thinking Is Still Required

80/20 delivers such clear-cut guidance that you will doubtless be tempted simply to purge everything and everyone that ends up in Quad 4 with No Scrubs and Ain't No Mountain High Enough. It's a no-brainer, right?

The thing is, we are both blessed and cursed with brains and, often, it's good to use them. If you are certain you can never make money on a given B product, No Scrubs is the appropriate option. If you know you have a group of customers who need a certain B product and are willing to pay a profitable price for it, go ahead— make shameless use of Ain't No Mountain High Enough. But more complex situations call for the application of the more complex tools.

Transform Business Insights into Business Segments

Don't You (Forget About Me), for instance, is a complex tool that can extract a margin from some low-performing products sold to low-performing customers. Before dropping the product in question, try offering specials or making low-volume runs of the item on preannounced dates exclusively. By concentrating demand, you also concentrate the need for resources. Or you might apply the Time After Time approach to achieve this concentration. Collect, hold, and then pool orders of a low-performing product until you have enough orders to justify a special or low-volume run.

Often, simplifying an offered product simply means dropping it from your shelves or catalog or website. But tools such as My Way (reducing the variety of sizes or options) and You've Got Another Thing Coming (packaging the product with all its possible components or accessories) can transform a single-item sale into a multiple-item sale. Whichever option you choose, you'll end up with less drain and more profits.

And Think Some More

Now that you've learned how to think about simplification, keep thinking. Both customers and products are obvious targets for segmentation, but also look beyond these to your entire business. If it has both expanded and diversified, you need to ask, Do the various components of the business perform optimally with each other? Or has the company become a less viable business because it is now an agglomeration of dissimilar businesses? If the company's operational divisions are significantly dissimilar, your organization might have passed the point at which 80/20 can be meaningfully applied exclusively to products and customers. You might need instead to apply it to the various and varied segments of your business to guide you toward simplifications that will empower you to allocate your resources more effectively.

Once you have applied 80/20 to each business segment, consider simplifying the lower-performing business segments into business units more focused on fewer products and/or markets. Consolidating a business segment in this way enables simpler and yet more detailed and meaningful performance tracking. Simplification and more effective allocation of resources make it easier for a business to increase the unit's share of A customers.

It is not always obvious that a given business, subsidiary, or business unit requires simplification. Say, for instance, that one of your businesses sells machine tools. These are high-cost capital products. It is almost natural that you would want to integrate into the company parts and service for those machines—and yet the business models, including sales, marketing, physical plant, and finance, are very different for a firm making capital-intensive products (big machinery) versus a firm selling service and parts. Viewed from the perspective of a consumer, putting machinery together with parts and service makes ample sense. But this might not be true when viewed from the perspective of the producer or manufacturer.

Apply segmentation to the business through 80/20. Perform separate quad segmentation for the capital products and the parts and services offerings. This will enable you to create meaningful profit and loss statements (P&Ls) for each segment of the business. You might decide that product type is not the only useful way to segment your business. Depending on the nature of a given company, a different type of segmentation strategy might be applied, including segmenting by customer types, market segments, or international geographies. Determine the most efficient criteria for using 80/20 to segment your business and then test your assumptions by running P&Ls for each segment you propose to elevate to a new subsidiary business. Comparing the result with your current analysis will determine how useful a segmentation strategy is for your business.

Transform Business Insights into Business Segments

Applying 80/20 is a great way to help you understand the customer, product, and segment performance of your current business, but you can also use it to sharpen your mind and stimulate your imagination to see—and possibly restructure—your business in an entirely new way for the future. This is the subject of the Chapter 4.

Chapter 4

Perform the Zero-Up Thought Experiment

Observation is a passive science, experimentation an active science.

> —Dr. Claude Bernard, *Introduction to the Study of Medicine*, 1865

Pareto's principle, which applies to pea plants and profitability alike, packs a punch approaching the inevitable force of a natural law. But does this mean that you and your business are doomed to 80/20 inefficiency, squandering 80 percent of your resources on serving the trivial many instead of the 20 percent of customers and products—the critical few—responsible for 80 percent of your revenue?

You can picture the Pareto principle as it applies to business as two pyramids, one upright, the other inverted, in Figure 4-1.

This illustrates the 80/20 distribution imbalance, in which 20 percent of customers/products produce 80 percent of revenue, and 80 percent of customers/products produce 20 percent of revenue. Grim indeed. But the late John D. Nichols Jr., CEO of Illinois Tool Works (ITW), introduced "overhead" as a third pyramid (see Figure 4-2).

Overhead consists of all fixed costs, costs that are necessary but that do not contribute directly to producing and selling a given product. What we see when the third pyramid is added is that your most profitable customer/product combinations not only produce

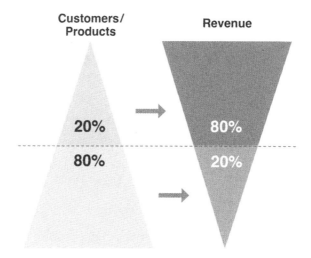

Figure 4-1 Pareto Principle (Without Overhead)

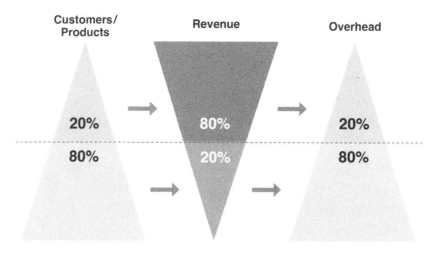

Figure 4-2 Pareto Principle (with Overhead)

80 percent of your revenue but are responsible for just 20 percent of your fixed costs. There is no imbalance here: 20 percent of your most productive customers/products consume 20 percent of your overhead. The equation balances, and thus, justice is done! Moreover, when it comes to the trivial many, the 80 percent of

customers/products who produce just 20 percent of your revenue consume 80 percent of your overhead. As a fixed cost, overhead is apportioned equally among customer/product combinations. The cost of overhead is the same for a profitable customer/product combination as it is for an unprofitable combination. It's just that, for accounting purposes, twenty critical customer/product combinations in effect consume twenty units of overhead, whereas eighty trivial customer/product combinations consume eighty units.

When we add overhead to the 80/20 equation, it becomes clear that squandering 80 percent of your resources to get just 20 percent of your revenue creates an even more dire situation than if you consider only the direct costs of customer/product combinations versus revenue.

Cheer up! The fixed status of overhead does not nullify the 80/20 Pareto principle. You can't nullify a law of nature. But the case of overhead does give you a hint about what you can do to tilt 80/20 powerfully to your advantage. It turns out to be a matter of simple math plus an exercise of the imagination.

What If?

What if your only customer/product combinations were the 20 percent that generated 80 percent of your revenue and required just 20 percent of your present overhead? In other words, imagine that all your customers and products were those in your Fort, Quad 1.

But what's the point in imagining this? After all, "If wishes were fishes, we'd have some fried, and if wishes were horses, beggars would ride." So, what *is* the point of this exercise?

One of the many scientific breakthroughs credited to Albert Einstein is the *Gedankenexperiment*, literally the "thought experiment." It is a bold technique for projecting the results of a what-if scenario, a future state that does not yet exist and might never exist. It is an exercise

Perform the Zero-Up Thought Experiment

of the imagination, to be sure, but it is also bounded by certain rules that transform it from a mere wish into a mental model or even a logical argument that is made within the context of a totally hypothetical scenario, even one that is radically counterfactual, clearly contrary to known facts. Nevertheless, however counterfactual, a thought experiment never descends into pure fantasy. Cause and effect still apply.

Right now, there's a high likelihood that roughly 20 percent of your customers and the products they buy are responsible for roughly 80 percent of your revenue. These customers, however, also account for just 20 percent of your overhead costs. Also right now, you have no choice but to foot 100 percent of the overhead bill, including the 80 percent that is effectively allocated to customers who produce a trivial fraction of your revenue, namely 20 percent. Add to these *fixed* costs the *direct* costs of making or acquiring all the SKUs you carry and the *direct* costs of selling them—selling them *all*, not just the 20 percent that produce 80 percent of your revenue but also the 80 percent that produce just 20 percent of your revenue.

Why not conduct a thought experiment based on the counterfactual that those 20 percent are your only customers and the products they buy are your only products?

The difference here between a wish and a thought experiment is the ultimate mathematical question an experiment demands: "What would it take to serve these critical few customers if they were my only customers?" The answer to this question will tell you how to optimally structure the business imagined in the thought experiment—that is, a business selling only the critical few products to only the critical few customers.

Let's outline the steps necessary to answering this question:

- **Step 1:** Segment your current business, your business as it is, to identify Quad 1, The Fort, the top 20 percent customer/product combinations that produce 80 percent of your revenue.

- **Step 2:** Look at the people you currently employ. The jobs of some are overhead functions, which are not directly related to acquiring, making, or selling your products. We won't focus on them at this point. Instead, look only at those who are directly involved in acquiring, making, or selling products or otherwise directly serving customers. Among this group, identify your top performers—roughly the top 20 percent. We will discuss how to make this identification shortly, because doing so is not quite as straightforward as it might sound. You might have quite a good idea of the top performers in your current organization, but the problem is that the current organization does not serve only the top 20 percent of its customer/product combinations. So, even if you know quite clearly what it takes to serve 100 percent of your customers, you don't yet know what it takes to *optimally* serve the 20 percent who matter most. But before we tackle this problem, let's continue outlining the steps toward answering, "What would it take to serve these critical few customers if they were my only customers?"

- **Step 3:** In the thought experiment, this step is simple. Having already identified the customer/product combinations that belong in your Fort, move into it all your top-performing employees who are directly involved in making, acquiring, or selling products so that they will now serve only your top-performing customer/product combinations.

- **Step 4:** Fire everyone else. (In your experimental thoughts only, of course!) Actually, don't fire *everyone* else. You still need employees whose work is not directly related to products and customers but is part of the cost of overhead. Buildings still need to be maintained, packages shipped and received, accounting done, IT kept humming, and so on. This said, for purposes of the thought experiment, you should be able to cut

77

Perform the Zero-Up Thought Experiment

your overhead considerably (but not entirely) to suit a company that is 80 percent smaller in size than it formerly was. Because this is a thought experiment, you can assume a perfect downsizing that will save you 80 percent on overhead.

- **Step 5:** Run the numbers for your company, now downsized to serve only the top performers. You will likely discover that your scaled-down company is producing a 200 percent profit or even more.

To be useful, any thought experiment must at some point confront reality. The assumption that stakeholders in any business would be happy with reducing their footprint by 80 percent is unrealistic. In fact, our thought experiment is very good at creative destruction, cutting away everything trivial and leaving only the critical nub. Some people do this with their personal household budgets. They list last month's expenses and then identify every expense item they could do without, retaining only the absolutely necessary. The result is a bare-bones budget for the next month. In some circumstances, the bare-bones approach is compulsory rather than optional. You don't redecorate your house if you can't pay the coming month's mortgage. But, in less dire circumstances, you probably want to budget for more than the bare bones. Maybe you really enjoy a few monthly trips to a favorite restaurant or watching movies offered by your streaming subscriptions. Perhaps you don't want to give up your gym membership. Even in this less dire scenario, however, whittling down to the essential expenses gives you a base from which you can build a more generous budget.

We call this *zeroing-up*. Even if you have never heard the term or used the process, I can assure you that you are more familiar with zeroing-up than you think. Many of us really do zero-up our household budgets—or at least harbor a guilty feeling that we should be doing this. The truth is that most *successful* family budgeting begins when someone in charge finally asks, "How much money do we need for the month?" The month about to begin is the segment on which the budgeter focuses, and the question is answered by starting from a zero-dollars base. That is why this form of budgeting is called *zero-up* or *zero-based budgeting*.

You start with zero, and then add up the individual costs of what is needed for this month. When you have your total, you compare it to what you are going to take in for the month. Resolve the difference between the projected outlays and projected income by either sub-tracting from your spending (which probably means subtracting some or all your wants while leaving in place only your needs) or by adding to your income. Come next month, you do a new zero-up. You rinse and repeat throughout the year. I have never heard of anyone attempting to make a zero-up household budget for the next five or ten years, let alone for their entire projected lifetime. But, month by month, it is quite doable. Zeroing-up for your business, starting from the ground up, building a budget, and allocating resources from zero, is typically done on an annual basis, with quarterly reviews and corrections.

The zero-up thought experiment presents a counterfactual picture of how shedding 80 percent of your underperforming customer/product combinations produces a virtually frictionless business in which close to 100 percent of inputs prove to be close to 100 percent critical instead of 20 percent critical and 80 percent trivial. Starting from this point, zeroing-up helps you to determine just what it would take to *acquire* more A-customer/A-product combinations and also to move more B-customer/B-product com-binations up from Quads 2–4, promoting these to A status.

In a nutshell, the objective of zeroing-up is to simplify the company by de-resourcing customer/product combinations with poor profitability while over-resourcing those with meaningful, impactful profit share to gain. Done consistently, this will restructure the business such that your profit and loss (P&L) losers will be de-resourced and your P&L winners will be over-resourced. The losers are those that have no meaningful profit share to gain. Resources allocated to these are therefore largely squandered. The winners, by contrast, do have a pathway to gaining share. Resources allocated to the winners make the win even greater.

A 100 percent Quad 1 business does not exist in the real world, but you should act as if creating such a business were a realistic goal. Operate from this mindset, and you will attract, create, and retain more A customers as well as promote more B customers to A status. This, in turn, will sell more products, a fact that will likely promote your higher-performing B products to A status.

Zeroing-up is a process for guiding leaders to establish (or reestablish) the *necessary* level of resources to serve the critical few in preference to the trivial many. The goal is to reduce or eliminate the destructively disproportionate volume of scarce resources required to serve underperforming and nonperforming products and customers, especially in the lowest customer/product quad, Quad 4.

Refocus Resources

Establishing or reestablishing the *necessary* level of resources to serve the critical few in preference to the trivial many requires refocusing resources. This includes employees. To the extent possible, you must deploy or redeploy your top-performing employees from Quad 4 to Quad 1 and, more selectively, to Quads 2 and 3. The high-performing customer/product combinations in Quad 1 must be overserved. To the extent that customer/product combinations in Quads 2 and 3 have meaningful profit share to gain (potential for promotion from B to A status), these might also be more selectively served by skilled consultative sales employees, but most of the business in these two quads should be conducted as transactionally as possible, preferably through self-service (especially e-commerce).

In some cases, it is sufficient to redeploy the forces you have on hand. In other cases, you might need to hire additional people. But much of the time, zeroing-up requires dismissing underperforming employees and dropping the underperforming products and customers they serve. You don't do this to punish underperformers but to improve or even rescue your company. The point to remember is that your underperforming customer/product combinations are making it difficult, maybe even impossible, to adequately serve your best customers. And if you are underserving your most profitable customers, you will not only lose them; you will neither create nor attract more of them. It is urgent that you reallocate resources from the bottom to the top to create or attract more A-level customers. These, after all, are your fully committed loyalists, your raving fans, and zero-up is the most accurate and efficient way of converting B customers to A customers and A customers into fanatics. Neither intuition nor magic is required, just data-driven strategic selling, serving the most profitable customers more effectively and curating lines of products and services that your A customers demand.

Methods and Processes

Zeroing-up is the next logical step after focusing and segmenting, though some managers feel that the basic 80/20 segmenting and focusing processes give them all the information they need. I believe, however, that taking the next step, to zero-up, gives you more data-driven guidance in turning the business around and positioning it to earn the right to grow. Zeroing-up gives you detailed insight into deploying resources to where they will have the most positive impact.

What businesses benefit most from zeroing-up? The answer is simple. It is those that are seemingly incapable of converting their B customers into A customers and A customers into stark raving fans.

These organizations tend to spin their wheels endlessly brainstorming over marketing and advertising. The truth is that there is no quick fix. Typically, the most effective turnaround is achieved by starting from scratch—not with the whole company, but segment by segment. Gather the data and work the data for the first segment you want to improve. Run 80/20 on it and use only the resources organically available to that segment. Start with zero and build only what is needed to support this one segment's set of customers and products. Working in this patient way, a segment at a time, tends to reveal the hidden costs of complexity while also highlighting areas in which costs can be reduced or removed. Focusing on a single segment takes the thought experiment into the real world. You learn how to optimally shift resources, de-resource the unproductive, and over-resource the highly productive. Focusing on one segment at a time allows for productive trial-and-error solutions that, as they prove themselves, can be scaled up through the entire company. You might want to focus on a market segment, a product segment, a region, a business unit. Think in terms of proof of concept, of building models or prototypes that can be applied to larger segments of the company or even the entire company.

Quad Zero-Up

Instead of focusing on a single segment or unit of the business, you might want to extend the thought experiment in which you focused exclusively on Quad 1. Having already zeroed-up your Fort, creating P&Ls for it as if it were the entire business, do the same for Quads 2 and 3, creating P&Ls for each, as if each were the whole business.

Your objective in each of these three separate quads is to build a P&L that shows how to optimally run each without regard to the others. In creating each of these scratch-built quads, keep track of the spend required and the headcount. When finished, you will have produced three separate optimal future-state P&Ls for each quad, along with the headcount needed to support each quad and a running total. Assemble the three quads into the company. As for Quad 4, simplify it until you can wring some profit out of it.

Product/Customer Inflection Point Zero-Up

The most labor-intensive approach to zero-up begins by making a top-down list starting with the highest revenue–producing customer/product combination at the top and descending to the lowest at the bottom. Although this simple list ranks customer/product pairs by revenue, the true measure of success is profit. If you can determine who your profitable customers are, you can over-resource them sufficiently to make them your raving fans. Not only do you want to retain these customers, you also want to convert more A customers to raving status and more B customers to A status. To do this, you must perform an inflection point zero-up analysis to find the line that separates profitable from unprofitable customers.

Venture back into thought-experimental territory. Imagine you are the head of a newborn company. Take hold of the top-down customer list you have drawn up from your real company's data. Grab hold of your best customer—number one on the list—and move that customer to the newborn company. Next, calculate the bare minimum cost required to support this one customer. Factor in material costs, variable payroll, variable manufacturing overhead, fixed manufacturing overhead, selling, general, and administrative (SG&A) expenses, and other attached costs until you reach the earnings before interest, taxes, depreciation, and amortization (EBITDA) for that one best customer.

Now, turn back to your list, take from it the number two customer. Perform the same calculations you made for customer number one.

You know where this going, right? Clear down to the bottom of your list. What you will end up with is the EBITDA for each customer as well as a running total. What you will discover is that, as successively lower-performing customers are added to the list, the running-total EBITDA for this new company increases at a decreasing rate. If you plot the cumulative EBITDA graphically, you will produce a rather lumpy bell curve, rising, fluctuating somewhat, and flattening out.

You will also find that—at some point—the curve will inflect obviously downward. This marks the inflection point at which *adding* lower-performing customers lowers the company's overall EBITDA. Generally, each customer added beyond this inflection further lowers overall EBITDA. There might be a few exceptions to this general rule. You will likely find a few customers on the lower end of the list who contribute positively to EBITDA, and you might also find, on the high end of the revenue scale, some customers who violate the general rule that the more productive a customer is, the more profitable. In any case, when your list and curve are complete, reorder your customers strictly by their EBITDA, so that you have a true bell curve without hills and valleys. This done, find the peak of the curve. Everything to the right of the summit represents customers who eat away at your company's profitability.

You will discover something even more remarkable. The 80/20 principle holds that 80 percent of your revenue comes from just 20 percent of your customer/product combinations, but this 20 percent is responsible for significantly more than 80 percent of your profits, typically 150–200 percent.

Red, Yellow, Green

Both quad zero-up and customer inflection point zero-up are excellent starting points for executing an 80/20 simplification.

Although customer inflection point zero-up offers both a reasonable degree of depth even as it provides the satisfyingly decisive feeling some folks get from swiping right or swiping left on a dating app, a curve is ultimately a curve and not reality in all its granularity. Fortunately, you are not obliged to blindly obey either quad zero-up or zero-up based on the customer inflection point.

First, bear in mind that simply dropping customers and products is a target useful for target practice, but in the real world, you don't always want to hit the bull's-eye. Start with the zero-up results, but don't just go in for the kill. Chapter 3 has provided the dirty dozen, a full menu of strategic alternatives to the firing squad.

Second, consider subjecting the results of 80/20 segmentation and simplification to one more calculation, one that will yield an additional diagnostic indicator. I call it the *right to grow ratio*, and calculating it for businesses, business units, product lines, or other segments within your business or within an 80/20 quad yields red/yellow/green traffic signals that will help you decide how to treat a given area of your business.

To obtain the right to grow ratio for a given business segment, divide that segment's material margin by its total employee costs.

- Material margin is calculated by subtracting material cost and net freight from net revenue.
- Total employee costs encompass payroll, plus taxes, benefits, travel, commissions, bonuses, insurance, and so on.

The right to grow ratio is a straightforward measure of how a business segment converts inputs to outputs. It informs your zero-up actions with respect to earning the right to grow (see Figure 4-3).

Perform the Zero-Up Thought Experiment

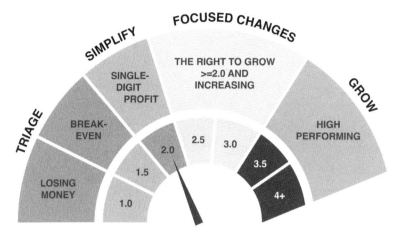

$$\text{Right to Grow Ratio} = \frac{\text{Material Margin}}{\text{Total Employee Cost}}$$

Figure 4-3 The Right to Grow Ratio

On a four-point scale:

- 3.0–4 (or greater) indicates a segment that should be over-resourced to achieve growth. This is a green light.

- A result between 2.0 and 3.0 indicates that the segment should be sufficiently resourced to move it toward growth—for example, by promoting a B customer/product combination to A status, which moves the combination from Quad 2 or 3 to Quad 1. This is a yellow light—proceed toward growth with caution.

- 2.0 indicates a segment with a potential for low double-digit profit.

- 1.5 indicates a segment with a potential for single-digit profit.

- 1.0 indicates a loser—that is, a segment with little or no potential for profit.

- 2.0 down to 1.0 is a red light. If the margins here cannot be improved, the segment should be dropped.

What Now?

What now indeed! Armed with the insight gained from applying 80/20 analysis and zeroing-up, you are positioned not yet to earn the right to grow but to articulate the *what* that will put you in position to earn the right to grow. What's the *what*? It is the goal toward which the business will aim all its efforts for the next three to five years, and it is best articulated in the language of business, which is money. That financial articulation is the subject of Chapters 5–8.

Chapter 5

Go Get a Goal

Climb high
Climb far
Your goal the sky
Your aim the star.

—Motto inscribed on the Hopkins Memorial Steps at
Williams College,Williamstown, Massachusetts

Chapters 2–4 presented the most important concepts, processes, and tools that will equip you to power through the four steps (Chapters 5–8) that, in the span of a hundred days, will position your business to earn the right to grow. This chapter lays out Step 1: Go Get a Goal.

You can't get around it: your business does need a goal. I get it. I know what it's like to feel overwhelmed at the very thought of setting a goal. The range of possibilities and pitfalls can close in on you like a heavy fog. Even worse is when the range of options seem shriveled into near nonexistence. Decision paralysis is especially common when it comes to setting life, career, or career/life goals. True, the fortunate few figure out early on what they want in life and career, but the majority agonize. Maybe for years.

Well, I come to you bearing good news. It is much easier to set a goal for a business than it is to set a life goal for yourself. If you don't believe me, just stick around.

The big difference between a life goal and a business goal is that the first might require some sort of spiritual or metaphysical self-examination whereas the second requires nothing more than some fluency in the language of business, which is the language of money. Take Christopher Columbus. We've been taught that he was an intrepid mariner moved by a passion for discovery. Proof of this was his audacious self-proclaimed goal of finding a "new world." You must admit that's a hell of an ambitious goal. Elon Musk set the goal of colonizing Mars. Ambitious? Yes. But the difference is that we know Mars exists, we know where it is, and we've even sent robotic explorers to its surface. Nobody knew if there was any new world west of the old, so Columbus's goal was quite the flyer.

Except that finding a new world was not his goal. No, Columbus had, in fact, a straightforward business goal, and he always framed it to potential backers in the language of business. In his day, the fifteenth and early sixteenth centuries, the breakthrough must-have products were gold and spices—with spices giving gold a real run for its money. Spices made foods infinitely tastier, of course, but, more important, in an age long before refrigeration and artificial preservatives, spices were essential to making food last longer by retarding spoilage and even making that food reasonably palatable after spoilage was under way. (You could use a load of salt for this purpose, but the problem with that was, whatever the food in question, salt tasted exactly like salt. Like salt, spices retarded spoilage. Unlike salt, spices enhanced flavor. In marketing, we call this a *relevant differentiator*.)

Spices were both a luxury and a necessity, which made them a high-value, high-demand product. The problem was that the most potent and desirable spices came from places very far from Europe and generally required pretty much circumnavigating the globe with an ocean voyage from Atlantic to Pacific waters. Typically, this meant going all the way around the Cape of Good Hope and back again at the tip of South Africa. Perpetually assailed by violent weather and roiling seas, the Cape passage was the most dangerous part of what was already an arduous and costly endeavor. Christopher Columbus, however, was familiar with a theory from a Florentine astronomer named Paolo dal Pozzo Toscanelli, who believed that the shortest route to the gold and spices of the East was to sail west. Columbus grabbed this innovation and took it to one prospective investor after another.

As schoolchildren, many of us were taught that people in the late fifteenth century believed the earth was flat and that if you sailed too far in any direction, you would fall off the edge. Among the uneducated masses, many, perhaps most, believed this. Among the educated and literate, however, it was commonly accepted that the earth was at least more or less a sphere. That was one key to the viability of Columbus's proposition to the venture capitalists of his era—the crowned heads of wealthy seagoing kingdoms. The other key was a belief that even if some mass of land got in the way before you reached the East, there must be a water passage through this barrier separating the Atlantic and the Pacific, what many called a passage to India.

So, Columbus's business goal was simple. It was to find a more direct, much faster, much safer westward route to the spices and gold of Asia, either by landing smack-dab on the shores of India or China or Cipango (Japan) or by locating a direct water passage to them. The monarch whose mariner achieved this first would be in position to enjoy a first-entrant advantage and could corner the market on spices and gold. The proposition did, however, prove to be a hard sell. One rich royal or noble after another turned Columbus down. At last, he was able to get an audience with King Ferdinand and Queen Isabella of Spain. This pair got it. They grokked Columbus's business goal because it was set in the language of business—money—and they very much liked money.

Follow Columbus

The life story of Christopher Columbus (1451–1506) and the story of his four voyages are complex, but his business goal was always direct, simple, and clear. It was to become wealthy by making his investors wealthy by enabling them to capture a competitive edge in what were by far the two most attractive markets of his age: the market for spices and the market for gold.

Your life and even the myriad details of your business might likewise be complex, which is all the more reason to follow Columbus in creating business goals that are direct, simple, clear, and defined by measurable goals. The most compelling measurable goal consists of stacks and stacks of cash. So, express your goals in the simplest of all languages: money. The private equity (PE) company that installed me as CEO of a troubled company it had acquired—again, let's call that firm Rolling Thunder Engineered Parts—spoke that language and expected me to do the same. I, in turn, led the executive leadership team of the company in speaking it as fluently as possible.

Setting a goal in terms of money is remarkably straightforward. Achieving that goal, however, requires careful analysis, tough decisions, unshakable commitment, hard work, and hard thinking. The first step, however, is simply to size the prize by answering two financial questions: Where are you now and where do you want to be in three to five years? Why three to five years? Some companies work on a three-year business plan, others prefer five. Doubtless, still others embrace a different time frame. In the case of the firm I was tasked to lead, our PE sponsor set a goal that was typical of many PE firms: to produce at least a three times multiple on invested cash (MOIC) within five years. Setting this goal is merely a matter of doing the math to calculate what earnings before interest, taxes, depreciation, and amortization (EBITDA) you need to score that three times

MOIC within the five-year time frame. For my company, it was a whole-of-company goal of $2.5 billion in revenue with high teen percentage margins and $300 million in EBITDA by year five.

I was leading a hundred-day program to position the company to earn the right to grow—that is, to set it on course to achieve profitable growth capable of reaching the year-five goal that had been set. Setting that goal required first understanding the present state of the business. Chapter 1 talked about what this involves at this early point in the first hundred days:

1. Gather and analyze the necessary data to determine your current EBITDA.

In addition, we needed to identify any obvious and urgent existential problems. If your house is burning, put out the fire. If your boat is leaking, plug the holes.

In the case of Rolling Thunder, we were operating under a specific mandate from our PE sponsor, which was to achieve three times MOIC within the five years. So, before setting our goal, we had to do the following:

2. Multiply by three the number we arrived at in action number 1.

3. Take the product of the multiplication in action 2 and present it as our goal, which was to reach $2.5 billion in revenue with high teens margins and $375 million in EBITDA within five years.

The data we needed to understand the present state of the business was superficial financial data. You could read it in an annual report and recent quarterly statements. Later, we would need to achieve a genuine situation assessment, which means a deep understanding of the business. But under the gun of a hundred-day timetable, we just needed enough on which to get a goal. Once we had this quick and dirty understanding, all we required was the first hour or so of the first hundred days to set the goal. I don't know how long it took Columbus to set the goal that Ferdinand and Isabella snapped up and that sent him on the four voyages spanning 1492–1504 that transformed the history of civilization by opening the way for European exploration, conquest, and colonization of the Americas. Nevertheless, I wouldn't be surprised if even his goal-setting time frame could be measured in mere hours, perhaps a number of them sleepless.

An unaimed arrow, they say, never misses. But it also, by definition, never hits a strategic—that is, intended—target. Does it take a serious archer long to pick a target? No. It's usually a bull's-eye that is in full view. It might not be easy to hit. There are multiple factors that influence the flight of an arrow, including wind conditions, the quality of the bow and arrow, and the strength, skill, judgment, talent, and concentration of the archer. No, it might not be easy to hit, and there are certainly no guarantees of success, but the bull's-eye itself is unambiguous. The loosed arrow either sticks it or doesn't. And when it doesn't? Confucious said, "When the archer misses the center of the target, he turns around and seeks the cause of his failure in himself." The miss is data. Use it in seeking the cause of the failure. Then correct *your* aim accordingly.

The financial goal we set for Rolling Thunder implied a more immediate goal, an intermediate goal, namely, taking needed steps to turn the business around, putting it in the best position to earn the right to grow. The first of those steps was to simplify the existing business by applying 80/20 (as set out in Chapters 2 and 3) to the same data sources as what were used to determine the company's current EBITDA. That rapid 80/20 analysis gave the executive team the information it needed to specify what business activities to immediately stop, start, or continue in order to begin the simplification of the business and thereby put a firmer footing under the company. As more data was acquired through time, the simplification process would continue and be refined so that the business was guided through a strategic growth transformation as the analyzed data showed us where to grow and where to raise prices with the single purpose of increasing the organization's profit.

Gap Analysis

If your company is owned by a sponsor, as was the case with the firm I led, you are blessed. Effectively, your goal is found in your contract. You just need to do the math. If you and your company are not thus blessed, setting your goal will likely take more time and effort. Still, if you are under pressure to earn the right to grow, you and your leadership team will need to move as quickly as possible to agreement on your company's three- or five-year goal.

Your decision-making can be greatly accelerated by adding a gap analysis to the initial rapid 80/20 analysis. It's difficult to write any business book without quoting Yogi Berra, legendary longtime manager of the New York Yankees and the most-quoted baseball celebrity of all time. Among his many quirkily oracular pronouncements was this: "We're lost, but we're making good time." To which we might add another Yogi-ism: "If you don't know where you are going, you'll end up someplace else." The tautological definition of *being lost* is *not knowing where you are*. If you do not know where you are, you cannot know where you *are* going, let alone *should* be going. So, gather the financial data you need to determine the present state of your company: *where you are*. Define this in the language of business: current revenue, current margin, current EDITDA.

Now that you are no longer lost—you know where you are—decide where you want to be in three to five years, again expressing this in terms of revenue, margin, and EBITDA. You can compare the current state to past performance to better inform a reasonable expectation of your future state three or five years hence. This reasonable expectation might make for a satisfactory goal or it might be insufficient. So, don't be afraid to make the goal more ambitious, taking into account an understanding of economic and other external conditions and the general expectation of your markets and your industry.

Right now, whether your goal derives from a PE sponsor or from the first steps of your 80/20 analysis and gap analysis, you have a goal and you have the dimension of the gap separating your present state from your desired future state. The remainder of the first hundred days will, among other things, complete the gap analysis. This involves the following steps:

1. Identify the objectives that you need to achieve to reach your future-state financial goal.

2. For each of the future-state objectives you identify, analyze the present state of these objectives. What is being done currently in each of these areas?

3. Figure out what you need to do differently from what you are doing today to successfully bridge the gap between the present state and the desired future state (i.e., your goal).

Among the many tried and tired cliches of business management is the expression "move the needle." The truth is that cliches become cliches because they *do* express some meaningful concept. Once you know where you are and where you want to be, as defined by the numbers, your task is to determine just what decisions and actions will *move the needle* from the present-state numbers to the desired future-state numbers. The most effective tool you have for bridging this gap is the strategic application of 80/20 analysis (see Figure 5-1).

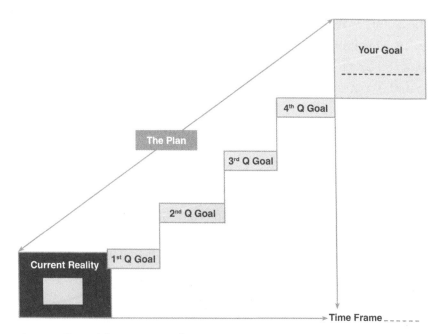

Figure 5-1 The Gap Analysis

Don't Sweat the Numbers

Data is the essential basis for all strategically valid decision-making. That is, there is no strategy without adequately interpreted data. Yet, in setting your goal, I advise you not to sweat the numbers beyond a rapid 80/20 analysis and a gap analysis. Let me explain.

The most important thing about the goal that kicks off the first hundred days is not how you arrived at the numbers in that goal. The most important thing is that the goal is *a goal*. Before you had a goal, you didn't have a goal. And without a goal, you had no target, no aspiration, no marker of a future that is better than the present. The numbers? They do have a basis in data, and they might well be exactly the right numbers. But, then again, maybe better numbers could have been chosen. One thing is for certain: they are not the *wrong* numbers. How do I know this? Because they are aspirational.

The numbers that make up our goal do not represent factual reality. As an aspiration, the numbers that define our goal have yet to be achieved as facts. They are aspirations. True, to constitute a good goal, the numbers need to be at the very least possible and preferably feasible. (The 80/20 and gap analyses will go a ways to ensuring that.) Yet the aspirations should also be ambitious. "A man's reach should exceed his grasp," the poet Robert Browning wrote, and that's good advice for anyone seeking to earn the right to grow.

To sum up, a good goal makes a good target. We don't need to measure the millimeters in the diameter of the bull's-eye. It's a bull's-eye, maybe a little too big, maybe a little too small, maybe just right. No matter. It gives us something to aim our arrow toward. It provides a direction, and when you are trying to get an urgent move-on, you need first and foremost a direction.

When your leadership task is to position an underperforming company for profitable growth—that is, to turn it around so that it is aimed at earning the right to grow—you yourself might feel conflicted. As the CEO, you are expected to have all the answers. Of course, the one thing you do know for certain is that you do *not* have all the answers. You need to learn more about the company and its people in action and over time before you can begin to get all the answers you need. Right now, however, what you do have to offer is a process. You do not have all the necessary answers, but you possess a process that will lead the organization in gathering the data, applying valid analytical processes to that data, setting a goal, and transforming analysis into action. You will lead the enterprise to improvement, not perfection. Whatever else your tenure might be, it will always be a work-in-progress. If you make the mistake of buying into the CEO mystique—the idea that you alone can fix it—you will not be prepared to look and listen so that you can understand the culture of the company and absorb the salient features of its history, its processes, and its expectations.

Get to the Dentist Before You Hit an Iceberg

Have you ever bitten into a sweet, juicy apple and felt a sharp twinge in a tooth? Is your first action to speed dial your dentist? I don't think so. Your first response is denial. *It will pass*, you assure yourself but, just to make sure, you eat the rest of that apple far more gingerly. Eventually, when part of the tooth breaks off, your exposed nerve finally drives you to the dentist.

In business, most signs of decline are at least as obvious as an ache in a tooth. Glancing over several quarters of numbers tells the tale. As with the tooth, the indication is clear, but denial is still possible. At Rolling Thunder, the downward slide was undeniable. But had I been built a bit differently, I could still have found a way to deny it because, on my arrival at that company, I also saw a slew of projects and initiatives under way. There was a lot of activity. People looked busy. I could have sighed with relief: *Well, they're not giving up, are they? With all this activity, there's hope yet. Something good has got to happen!*

I did sigh, but that response was not born of relief. I knew from experience that declining revenues and shrinking margins are often accompanied by a hopeful profusion of products and a desperate hum of activity. To me, the buzz was an alarm. Churning out products unaccompanied by strategic consideration of return on investment is not just *not good enough*, it is *not good at all*. It bleeds money. The more you churn it out, the more it bleeds. It did not take much more digging to see that nobody at the firm was paying much attention to cash flow. Other essentials—financial data, analytics, key performance indicators, and tracking capabilities were weak and, in some instances, totally missing. Tax issues, including add-back limitations, severance obligations, and contractual cash requirements, were not being tracked and analyzed. Yet it was clear that these were taking their toll on a decaying cash situation. Still, I detected no attempt to reverse the trends.

What sunk RMS *Titanic* on April 14–15, 1912? Collision with an iceberg. That's certainly not the wrong answer, so you do get partial credit for it. But if you want an A, you need to come up with more:

- The ship's highly experienced captain, Edward J. Smith, was aware that icebergs were in the vicinity, but he did not moderate his speed accordingly. His focus was not on the likely presence of bergs but on his intense desire to better the transatlantic crossing time of *Titanic*'s sister ship, *Olympic*. Avoiding collision with an iceberg should have been a prime strategic objective. Instead, Smith allowed himself to become distracted by a nonstrategic objective.

- Captain Smith also failed to ensure that he would receive all updates on any icefields he might encounter. The still-new technology of wireless (radio) communications was being used to transmit regular ice warnings to ships in the area, including *Titanic*. These warnings poured in, but the messages were not prefixed with the initials MSG—Masters' Service Gram—which marked them as something to be delivered immediately to the captain (ship's "master"). Perceiving no urgency, the wireless operator set the warnings aside as routine messages and did not deliver them to the bridge. Because the ship was nearing its destination, New York City, the operator was inundated with messages his passengers wanted delivered immediately. He made those his first priority. He should have known better and ensured that the captain received the updates. But, then, Smith himself should have given him instructions to bring him all ice warnings, with or without the MSG prefix. Ensuring the prompt delivery of vital data should have been regarded as what it most certainly was, strategically critical, essential to carrying out the main imperative of sailing strategy, namely, don't wreck the ship by hitting something.

- It was approaching midnight as *Titanic* ventured through the icefield. The night was cold and clear—no fog—and the sea was calm. But it was still dark, of course, and the calm sea meant that there were no telltale waves breaking against the icebergs, which made them harder to detect. Well, that's what lookouts equipped with good binoculars are for. Except that the ship's stock of binoculars was locked up at night, and the lookouts didn't have them. Good binoculars are expensive optical instruments, and you don't want them growing feet and walking off. Nevertheless, antitheft precautions are far lower on the strategic spectrum than ensuring your lookouts have the equipment they need to see danger, especially in hazardous waters, especially at night.

- It is possible that the system of command communication within the ship was fatally flawed. A clear, quick, unambiguous system of command communication is of self-evident strategic importance, and yet, the *Titanic*'s helmsman might have made the wrong turn in response to an ambiguous emergency command. According to a story passed down from the granddaughter of a *Titanic* officer who survived the wreck, as soon as the iceberg was seen, the command was given to turn "hard a-starboard." As it was relayed to the helmsman, however, the order was misinterpreted as a command to turn right rather than to push the tiller right to turn the ship to the left. The error was discovered, but valuable seconds had been lost, and it was too late to correct course.

- There is evidence that the crew did not fully understand the effects of one of *Titanic*'s principal innovations, its three-screw propulsion design (most ships of the period had just two screws). When the ship's first officer ordered the engine room to put the engines in reverse as a means of slowing the ship, both the starboard and port screws turned backward, but, by design, the rotation of the central screw could not be reversed,

Go Get a Goal

only stopped. Because the central screw was the steering screw, its being stopped dramatically reduced the vessel's ability to turn smartly. The failure to understand basic aspects of the ship's technology worked against the essential strategic objective, which was to steer away from collision.

The *Titanic* disaster was not an instance of misfortune. It was a failure both to articulate a strategy and to execute on the very core of the core strategy of commanding a craft: Don't wreck the ship. This was the case with the company I was sent to reposition to earn the right to grow. There was no compelling, controlling strategy. There was a lot going on, but none of it was pulling toward a common strategic goal. It was like the *Titanic*'s three screws. Their operation was not managed in a coordinated manner to achieve the imperative goal. Instead, one was working against the other two.

At my company, the only thing that was crystal clear was that the business was running out of gas. Setting a goal was not only necessary, it was also the quickest incentive to formulating a strategy and then aligning around it. The subject of my first core meeting with the upper management team was to set a goal capable of turning the company around. That goal, that target, was the seed from which the strategy would have to grow. The first action step in the strategy that immediately followed from the goal was to identify the segments of the company that were hurting—indeed, killing—us, so that they could be either priced up to earn their keep or jettisoned as toxic. 80/20 would show us the way.

The goal itself? It was at most plausible. We had no reason to believe that we would absolutely achieve it, but we had a direction and a set of numbers that showed us our go-get: what we needed to achieve or obtain to move toward the goal.

Step 1 is all about inertia, that property of mass Sir Isaac Newton defined in his first law of motion: objects at rest possess a tendency to remain at rest. Objects in motion possess a tendency to remain in motion. The presence of a goal gave us a destination and direction so that the organization began to move in a strategic direction and toward a strategic destination. As a direct result of Step 1, the business was at last in productive, controlled motion.

Strategy Is Profitability and Profitability Is Strategy

Looking at the numbers of the company I had come to lead, you would be tempted to say that the one thing it lacked was profitability. This assessment is true as far as it goes, but it also misses a more essential lack. What the company did not have was an effective strategy. It had many companies, divisions, and products operating without coordination of purpose. It had grown, and a lot of people in the organization wanted to add to that growth. The thing is, although *strategic* growth is always good, growth in itself can turn out good (sometimes the dice come up in your favor), but, more likely, non-strategic expansion (you can't really call it *growth*) produces more costs without commensurate profits. And that is anything but good. When I came into the business, the year's first quarter showed normalized revenue down and normalized EBITDA down even more. Looking at April sales, this downward trend was getting worse.

I had already spoken with enough of the company's people to know they were intelligent and committed. They weren't very happy, which I took as an encouraging sign that they were not divorced from reality. But they had gotten to the point where they were by failing to pay enough attention both to the business and to one another. They were not acting in concert. Some pushed one way, others pulled in a different direction. Many were just trying to remain in place. Getting a goal was the first step in bringing alignment and concerted effort.

The company was diverse, a quality that, on balance, is more positive than not. But I reflected on something I noted in Chapter 1: people go into business for different reasons. Some are passionate about this or that industry or product line. Some simply take their preordained place in a family business. For others, there is an ethical or even philanthropic imperative. My employers, PE, are, of course, investors. Their business purpose is straightforward. They acquire a business for what they consider a low price—that is, for a value capable of being added to and then sold at a profit—which means that their reason for doing business is to make money. Buy low, add value through profitable growth, and sell the resulting company. I guess I am biased, but I think of this model as a very pure business model. It is at the heart of most successful businesses, which transform something into something else of greater value which they subsequently sell for an even greater value. Adding value to profit from that added value benefits all stakeholders in the enterprise. Let there be capitalism, and you will see that it is good.

But it only works if every aspect of the transformation is strategic. I'm not a big fan of synonyms. I try to use exact language. If something is *enormous*, I don't call it *big*. As Mark Twain said, "The difference between the almost right word and right word is really a large matter—it's the difference between the lightning bug and the lightning." Yet I'm here to tell you that, in business, there is great power in thinking of the words *profitability* and *strategy* as synonyms. They need to be inseparable. Profitable growth *is* strategic growth. As for mere growth, better to call it *expansion* or, better still, *bloat*. It is to be avoided like the costly plague that it is.

Presenting the Goal

At my first core meeting with the executive leadership team of Rolling Thunder, I allocated ten days of my first hundred days to setting a five-year goal for the company. Virtually every one of these days was devoted to gathering and analyzing data to nail down the present state of the company. (Recall Chapter 1 and Chapter 2.) Coming up with the definition of the desired future state, our goal, took perhaps ten or fifteen minutes of calculation. Writing out the single-sentence result—"Reach $2.5 billion in revenue, have high teens margins, and $375 million in EBITDA within five years"—took maybe ten seconds.

Almost immediately after the leadership core meeting in which the goal was set, I convened our first town hall meeting to present the goal to a gathering of some fourteen hundred employees. At both the town hall and in a summary open letter to the company following it, I explained: "We will begin by simplifying our business. The executive team has reviewed what to stop, start, and continue doing immediately to get foundationally solid; we will communicate that shortly." I also mentioned the 80/20 process, identifying it as our chief tool for analyzing our data "to determine where to simplify and where to grow the business by raising prices to increase our bottom line."

As mentioned previously, the town hall we held combined an in-person meeting and a virtual meeting because the participants were distributed over some forty locations in the United States and abroad. The town hall was scheduled for two hours. The first sixty minutes were dedicated to my delivering a status report on the present state of the company, followed by the goal that defined the target future state. I told the truth, the whole truth, and nothing but the truth. I told it with data and words interpreting the data. I used nouns and verbs, modified by as few adjectives and adverbs as possible. I did not scold. I did not editorialize.

In the back of my mind was that marvelous scene in the 1995 Tom Hanks classic *Apollo 13*, in which NASA engineers are tasked with finding a solution to replace the inadequate carbon dioxide scrubbers in the Apollo Lunar Excursion Module (LEM) before the three-man crew of the stricken spacecraft is asphyxiated. There are working scrubbers available in the command module, but they are square and not designed to fit into the round scrubbers in the LEM, in which the astronauts have been forced to take refuge. So, the problem is straightforward: how do you fit a square peg into a round hole?

NASA engineers at ground control gather together all the parts available to the astronauts in space. They dump three boxes of assorted oddments onto a table. "All right, people, listen up," the lead engineer says. He holds up a square scrubber filter in one hand. "We gotta find a way to make *this* fit into the hole for *this*," he explains, holding up a cylindrical scrubber filter in his other hand. It is a delicious example of bringing instant and perfect clarity to a crisis situation. It answers the first critical question—*What* needs be done?—leaving only the second critical question: *How* do we do it?

At the town hall, answering that second question was my task. I explained that we were missing sales targets and that our costs were increasing. That was the present problem. *What* did we need to do? "Take immediate action to start hitting our targets while reducing costs."

How would we do it? "We would act quickly to cut spending and initiatives that were not tied to revenue generation." And then I continued to the *why*: "This will enable us to focus on the most important priorities for our success." Finally, I returned to the *how*, making it more specific by outlining the four steps to earning the right to grow.

With this presentation ended, the entire second hour of the town hall was devoted to answering questions from the participants. The first hundred days are all about accelerating change, getting into position as quickly as possible to earn the right to grow. One of the most important things I needed to accelerate was my own understanding

From Panic to Profit

of the company. In the days leading up to the town hall, I asked our employees to complete a questionnaire, which you can find in Chapter 1. The responses to the prepared questions told me a great deal about the company from the ground up. They also gave the people on the ground an opportunity to ask me questions. The answers and the questions in these documents became the basis for the second sixty minutes of the town hall. Before we reached the end of the town hall, I made sure to open the floor to spontaneous questions.

Every Process Begins with a Goal

In business, you get to choose between chaos and process. When I walk into a troubled company, I offer a process that begins with a goal, quickly moves through an orderly sequence of actions that earn the right to grow, and then follows through using the same processes reiterated with the objective of continuous incremental improvement toward the goal set early in the first hundred days.

Your process needs to be sufficiently flexible to answer the demands of triage. As soon as emergencies are addressed, move on to the merely urgent: cut spending and any initiatives not tied to revenue generation so that your very best people can laser-focus on the 20 percent of products and customers that account for 80 percent of your revenue.

Early in the first hundred days, as soon as you have set your goal, invite your entire team to look, with you, to the future. "Over the next few days, weeks, and months," I promised our employees, "we'll implement many changes to secure this company's health." If it is important to keep your promise, it is even more important to make the promise in the first place. A promise of change gives those in a declining organization rational hope. They need to see that the goal is attainable, and they need to see how. That is where the process comes in. "These changes will be tied to my four-step system, which takes three to four months to complete." A *process* is better than a *plan* because it is a system, a set of principles and procedures that tell everyone involved what to do and how to do it. Presented in the context of a process, the principles and procedures are seen as products of a tested, proven method. A *plan* is better than no plan, but it cannot hold a candle to a *process*, especially one that is defined in sequential steps and time-lined over a specific period.

I ended Step 1 by putting some skin—*my* damn skin—in the game. I took ownership of "my" process and promised my accountability for its success. I knew I could not control everything, of course, but I also knew that I could absolutely control my own accountability.

Chapter 6

Frame the Strategy

Time is money.

—Benjamin Franklin, "Advice to a Young Tradesman," 1748

Austin Dobson (1840–1921) earned a good living as a functionary in the British Board of Trade, but he also made quite a respectable reputation as a poet. Today, however, almost no one remembers him, let alone reads him. His time came, and his time went. He, of all people, would have understood this, as one of his shortest poems, "The Paradox of Time" (1877), attests:

Time goes, you say? Ah no!
Alas, Time stays, we go.

The thing is, we don't have much time, not when we need to earn the right to grow. Time stays, we go. And that is why setting the goal in Step 1 should be given no more than ten days out of the first hundred, including time to make a quick assessment of the current state of the business. The faster you determine your *what*—what you are going to achieve—the sooner you can address your *how*: how you will achieve your *what*. Step 1 was *what*. Step 2 is *how*.

Defining the *what* as a number, a financial goal, saved a lot of time up front. It only makes sense to let numbers guide the framing of your strategy, your *how*. If the present state of business dictates that you must earn the right to grow, you know that what you need is first and foremost a turnaround strategy. The heart of such a strategy is simplification.

Go for the Marrow

"Simplify, simplify," Henry David Thoreau advised readers of his *Walden* in 1854. Fail to do this, and you will almost certainly end up frittering away your life on the trivial many instead of focusing on the critical few. Thoreau explained that he decided to live for a while in a little cabin in the woods because he "wished to live deliberately, to front only the essential facts of life, and see if I could not learn what it had to teach, and not, when I came to die, discover that I had not lived. . . . I did not wish to live what was not life, living is so dear."

That last word caught my attention. Thoreau lived in a time when people often used *dear* and *expensive* or *costly* interchangeably. Life is so precious—of such dear cost—that he did not want to waste his expensive lifetime on trivial matters, things that were not of life's essence. A powerful writer, Thoreau didn't use the word *essence*. Instead, he said that he wanted "to live deep and suck out all the *marrow* of life, . . . to cut a broad swath and shave close, to drive life into a corner, and reduce it to its lowest terms."

Suck out the marrow and discard the rest. This was a strategy for living. Simplify so that you can focus not on the trivial many but on the critical few. Now, according to Hindorf et al. ("EANM Dosimetry Committee Guidelines for Bone Marrow and Whole-Body Dosimetry," *European Journal of Nuclear Medicine and Molecular Imaging, 37(6)* (2010), 1238–1250), bone marrow comprises about 5 percent of total body mass in healthy adult humans. So, Thoreau, a *life* strategist, was setting a truly radical goal for his project of simplification—achieving a trivial-to-critical ratio of 95/5. Fortunately, we mere *business* strategists have a different philosophical economist to follow, Vilfredo Pareto, whose observational research revealed that the concept of a trivial-to-critical ratio is quite real but, at 80/20, it is significantly more forgiving than what Thoreau demanded of himself.

In Step 2, then, you frame a strategy based on simplification as calculated according to the 80/20 principle, using the tools in Chapters 2–4. First assess the current state of the business to determine what is working and what is not working so that you can move resources from *what is not* working to *what is*. 80/20 enables you to convert the descriptive language—*what is not working* and *what is working*—to a quantified division: the 80 percent of resources, products, and customers that have a trivial positive impact on profitable growth versus the 20 percent of these things that have a critical positive impact. Having made this division, the next action frames a simplification strategy that enables the business to allocate as close to 80 percent of its resources to serving the 20 percent of customers and products that produce 80 percent of its revenue.

The deliverable for Step 2 is the framework of a strategy to position the company to earn the right to grow. A hundred-day turnaround timeline goes by fast, so speed is of the essence. The sooner the turnaround begins, the sooner profitable growth can begin. Don't expect the draft of the strategy produced in the span of Step 2 to guide your business for all time. In fact, your objective at this point is merely to propel the business to Step 3, in which the executive and operational leadership puts some meat on the strategic bones and give the business a new structure going forward, one intended to enable, facilitate, and accelerate optimum focus on customers and products that drive profitable growth.

With the hundred-day clock ticking, Step 2 promises not perfection but progress. The strategy that emerges from Step 2 is not intended to be final but to be capable of modification going forward in response to both monitoring as well as the changing demands of reality. Use the 80/20 tools presented in Chapters 2 and 3, and add

115

Frame the Strategy

to these the zero-up procedure explained in Chapter 4. Combine all your 80/20 insights to repeat your assessment of what is working and what is not.

Win from Your Core

Good data is necessary to frame an effective strategy, but it is not sufficient. An 80/20 analysis identifies the products and customers on which to focus. Understand, however, that this information is not just about products and customers; it reveals the core of your business, which is a valuable strategic insight. Based on the goal set in Step 1, frame a strategy that over-resources Quad 1 and then treats the remaining quads proportionately. But also understand that, by doing this, you begin to shape a strategy that aims to win at your core. Step 2 decisions should play to the core strengths of the business as revealed by 80/20 and the zero-up process. Go beyond the numbers here to define the company's core strength in words. This will stimulate thinking and enable more accurate assumptions and predictions going forward.

There's an added benefit to describing the core. It stimulates innovation. If you frame the strategy strictly from data from current customers and products, you will inevitably frame a strategy for today. That is important to do, but if you also move beyond today's reality by framing a strategy based on current data plus a broader understanding of core strengths, you can point your way to a path of future innovation and continuous improvement.

The vision you develop of your core will doubtless take time to evolve. Therefore, frame your business's strategy on its core strengths, but, during the first hundred days, continue to prioritize the speed required to *earn* the right to grow. Speed in simplification almost invariably means a trade-off that sacrifices anything approaching perfection. It is unrealistic to expect that the strategic draft you create in a matter of days will guide the company for the full five years of a five-year plan.

Fortunately, that is not the job at hand. The strategic framework hammered together in Step 2 is analogous to the scaffolding rapidly built to enable the construction of a tall building. It is intended to get you not to the perfect strategy but merely to the next level, to Step 3, in which the executive and operational leadership of the business forms a viable and durable structure for the company as it moves forward. It is a structure intended to make tomorrow better than today by enabling, facilitating, and accelerating optimum focus on the core strengths of the company that will earn the right to grow by the end of the first full year in the execution of the turnaround strategy. The principal deliverable of Step 2 is a working plan meant to be modified by the impact of the real world as the company moves forward.

What Step 2 Looks Like

Step 2 lays out the major objectives and initiatives to achieve the goal set in Step 1. This requires translating the insights gained from the Step 1 goal setting into a strategic framework capable of creating a new business structure: the strategy itself. Step 2 typically unfolds in a series of meetings among members of the management team, who analyze the most recent data and compare it to data gathered over the prior year. The resulting picture reveals trends that should inform the decisions that will guide the strategic structure created in Step 3.

The Step 2 framework provides sufficient scaffolding to enable the leadership team to make informed decisions about the objectives that must be achieved to attain the long-term (three- to five-year) goal. With the objectives articulated, the strategic alignment of the organization can begin. You have five big questions to answer:

1. What is needed to achieve breakthrough growth and/or performance?
2. What are the differentiators required to win?

3. What are the strategic opportunities or issues? Consider, for example, new product development, line extension, acquisitions, and so on.

4. What are the highest-value opportunities? Consider, for example, the potential of new product lines and their affordability.

5. With questions 1–4 answered, ask and answer: *What are the critical few initiatives to prioritize?*

Work the Framework

The 80/20 framework positions managers to build a strategic business structure aligned with their highest critical few priorities. In my experience, these should be at least three (remember the rule of three) but no more than five. With alignment outlined, the next action is framing a cross-functional execution, which is a blueprint for building profitable growth. At this point, the focus is usually on organic growth, to the exclusion of mergers and acquisitions (M&A). Thus, the coordinated execution framework positions the team to move resources from less productive customer-product combinations to investment in growth through geographic and line expansion anchored in the business core, as we did in the case of the company Rolling Thunder. Strategic alignment is data-driven. Using the 80/20 tools presented in Chapters 2–4, the business is segmented into four quads:

Quad 1: The Fort. This quad matches A customers with A products they buy. It's placed in the upper left corner of your quadrant chart.

Quad 2: The Necessary Evil. This quad is for the B products sold to A customers.

Quad 3: The transactional business. This quad is for the A product combinations sold to B customers.

Quad 4: Price up or exit. B-customer/B-product combinations are relegated to this quad. It's a segment that must either be priced up or exited from.

Bear in mind the purpose of this segmentation, which is to strategically coordinate the allocation of resources in a way that optimizes each customer/product quad. Naturally, the optimization begins with and is based on ensuring that Quad 1, the fort, is the prime focus of resources. The 80/20 ratio is the product of a natural law of disproportionate distribution. Appropriately or adequately resourcing Quad 1 requires *over-resourcing* it. For instance, you might deploy to this quad a dedicated consultative sales team, direct phone line and email address, a consigned inventory, and anything else that treats these customers and products as your crown jewels. All people are created equal, but not all customers and the products they buy. In business, every customer must be treated fairly but not equally. Only after The Fort is appropriately over-resourced can the leadership team go on to strategically allocate and align the remaining available resources to Quads 2 and 3.

Quad 2 should be *sufficiently* resourced to serve the A customers who buy B products. This means allocating to these customers a level of service designed to retain them while pricing the B products to perform as well as B products can. Give due consideration to the nickname of this quadrant: the Necessary Evil. Allow equal weight to both words, *necessary* and *evil* so that you position this quad to retain your A customers while framing the strategy to either move current B customers up from the B ranks or attract and acquire more A customers from the outside.

For the B customers buying A products in Quad 3, the framework needs to align with a strategy of selling that requires minimal resources. This segment is therefore one of opportunistic sales. The

119

Frame the Strategy

business grows profitably on your 80s, the roughly 20 percent of product/customer combinations that produce 80 percent of your revenue. This does not mean that you should shun opportunistic business, provided that these sales can be made transactionally rather than through resource-intensive relationships. Quad 3 is not a place for inherently high-cost consultative selling. It is the place for low-cost e-commerce sales and other transactions involving minimal investment of resources.

This leaves Quad 4, the B-product/B-customer segment. Some strategic frameworks cut out this segment entirely. The business walks away from it. Generally, I believe the better way to treat it is to consider it a segment to price up or exit. Those product/customer combinations that can be profitably served using a creative combination of price increases, resource reduction, and sales restrictions (such as requiring minimum purchases, online sales only, credit/debit card purchases only, and so on—the techniques you learned called the *dirty dozen*) should be retained or at least given a chance. If a product cannot be sufficiently priced up, it must be dropped. It is too self-destructive to spend direct resources and overhead to perpetuate the loss of money. Of course, you will lose customers when you drop products that are irredeemable and unprofitable, but this will be a boon, not a loss to your organization.

Draft a Segmented Profit and Loss Statement (P&L)

Step 2 is a great opportunity to translate your segmented portfolio into a segmented profit and loss statement. Such a segmented P&L might look like this:

Quad 1: 64 percent of total revenue ➔ +>100 percent of total profit

Quad 2: 16 percent of total revenue ➔ break-even profit

Quad 3: 16 percent of total revenue ➜ +5-15 percent of total profit

Quad 4: 4 percent of total revenue ➜ −significant *loss* (It is killing you.)

What this view dramatically demonstrates is the significance of what a zero-up (Chapter 4) will tell you: a P&L is, of course, a statement of profit and loss, which means a combination of positive and negative numbers. Business is no different from arithmetic or algebra in that negative numbers are just as real as positive numbers. If your business had only Quad 1, you'd be running a greater than 120 percent of total profit. Add Quad 3 and you can push this up to more than 120 percent. But both these numbers are true only in your imagination, in the zero-up thought experiment. If this were your business, its present reality would also include Quad 2, which is a wash, neither positive nor negative, and Quad 4, a terrific loser at −120 percent. This P&L portrays the company as a four-cylinder car that is currently sputtering along on just one cylinder (Quad 1), with two (Quads 2 and 3) that just barely pulling their weight, and one (Quad 4) that is basically running in reverse.

A deeper-dive analysis is required to sort actual product categories (or even individual SKUs, stock-keeping units) into each quad so that the performance of the company's portfolio might be critically assessed at a granular level. This leads to a more meaningful discussion aimed at formulating an "80/20 charter," which answers the question, "What products/product categories are we going to retain to create an optimal portfolio?" In other words, *On what, exactly, will we focus?* But the segmented P&L you draft in Step 2 is not a time-consuming deep dive but a quick sketch. Nevertheless, it is sufficient to chart general trends, and this provides enough insight on which to base some plausible decisions resulting in reasonable actions. The real value of these actions is that they will produce measurable real-world results, meaningful data that can be analyzed to drive additional significant change in the days following the first hundred, when there is time and space for some deep dives. The decisions and actions formulated in Step 2 are unlikely to be anything close to perfect, but they are nevertheless necessary. Without them, you would have no data going forward on which to make new decisions and take course-correcting actions based on new information. In the first full business year that follows the first hundred days, you will modify your strategy and business plan. The framework produced in Step 2 is not something that *might* have to be modified. It is positively *intended* to be modified.

Frame the Cross-Functional Execution

Use the segmented P&L to frame a launch pad for the cross-functional execution of the strategy. Sketch an 80/20 picture of how simplification and focused sales growth will be applied over the next full year. This will enable your business to rise to Step 3, where you specify the actions that will optimally allocate approximately 80 percent of your resources to Quad 1. Step 2 will give you a leg up in this process.

Start by drawing additional human resources from Quad 4. Common sense might tell you that the greatest input of resources is needed in the quad with the most problems. The truth is that the biggest problem Quad 4 has is its toxicity to the rest of the business. You literally cannot afford to squander resources on customer/product combinations that are beyond redemption. Your goal for the rest of your organization is to reduce friction and increase efficiency across all functions:

- Formulate charters for each quadrant that specify its service level.

- Each charter can be used as a basis for quad-specific service-level agreements (SLAs) assigned to each quad.

- Ensure that charters and SLAs always, always, always over-resource Quad 1, thereby over-resourcing the A customers in The Fort.

- The Golden Rule? Align all value streams to Quad 1.

- Apply lean (see Chapters 8 and 11) and other efficiency and continuous improvement standards to all operations and processes. (These are specs only. They might be developed later in the first hundred days and can get more fully fleshed out and implemented during the first full year of strategic execution.)

- Add to your simplification task list a mandate to simplify your stable of vendors *if* it is apparent that consolidating vendors will secure the business volume pricing and thereby reduce costs.

- Specify improved inventory management with such practices as just-in-time and the like. (Again, the specs will require some time to develop and fully implement.)

Your segmented quad should scream out for *focused* sales growth efforts. Efficiently executing across functions requires aligning your go-to-market strategy with the priorities of the quads. Quad 1 must receive the most resource-intensive sales growth tactics, such as consultative selling and value-adding services such as white-glove delivery, installation, calibration—whatever is appropriate to your customers, industry, and markets. The other quads will have an increasingly transactional focus.

When you reach Step 2, you will likely view focused sales growth as a function of gaining market share and leveraging prices for profitable *organic* growth. Venturing beyond organic growth through M&A for geographic expansion and product line expansion might be considered in Step 2 if the goal set in Step 1 cannot be reached by organic growth alone.

Don't Be Afraid to Think Short Term

Strategy is an inherently long-term project. This does not mean, however, that short-term wins should be neglected or, even worse, scorned. On the contrary, now is the time to prioritize them. 80/20 analysis is strong on showing you the clearest path to success. We're not talking about reflexively lunging after low-hanging fruit, but you should use 80/20 to identify the product/customer combinations in your portfolio that promise sufficient juice to make a transactional squeeze worthwhile.

Winning is *good* anytime but feels *great* early in the game. It overcomes inertia, builds momentum, provides hope, and creates confidence. If your business consists of multiple companies, divisions, or discrete components, you can apply the early-win approach to them:

A. Division X supplies a commodity as a service and exhibits many of the focused qualities that give it the clearest path to rapid wins.

B. Division Y has a top-heavy, deeply entrenched administrative state with too damn many priorities (i.e., pet projects). The situation is not hopeless but needs work, and that work is not yet under way. Time is required before improvement will be demonstrated.

C. Division Z is competently run but sells into a mature market with a horizon already plainly visible. Consider closing this division or simplifying it for inclusion in one of the other divisions.

The action to take immediately? Allocate more resources to Division X, not because it is suffering—*it's not!*—but because it is doing very well as an 80s performer, a profit source that has already earned its right to grow.

Earn the Right to Grow Ratios

A common way to determine which company or component has the clearest path to success is to analyze earn the right to grow ratios. Typical ratios to look at include the following:

- **Working capital ratio:** Dividing current assets by current liabilities reveals how capable a company is of meeting current financial obligations.
- **Price-earnings ratio:** Dividing current stock price by earnings per share yields the price investors pay for $1 of a company's profit.
- **Return on assets:** Dividing net income by total assets reveals what percentage of profit a company earns versus its available resources.
- **Return on equity:** Dividing net income by shareholders' equity indicates how efficiently management uses investors' capital.

The Step 2 Work Product

The function of Step 2 is to advance the strategy-making process to Step 3, with an eye toward Step 4. For this reason, Step 2 should deliver clear conclusions:

- Where the organization will compete
- How the organization will compete
- What capabilities are required to compete
- Why the organization will win

Each of these conclusions must make sense in the context of these parameters:

- The goal set in Step 1 (that is, the numbers needed to position the business to earn the right to grow)
- The current mission and vision of the company
- Performance trends as embodied in historical data

Step 2 output should recommend strategic imperatives and priorities. Recognizing that the work of the first hundred days is to provide an executable course of action that not only enables modification and correction but contemplates these (it makes progress and does not pretend to achieve perfection), each priority and imperative should be defined in terms of rationale, scoping, and actual value-at-risk versus potential value-creation. A realistic and useful rule of thumb is to relate each strategic priority to three to five strategic initiatives aimed at earning the right to grow by the following:

- Strengthening the core (corresponding to the fort)
- Improving market attractiveness
- Improving competitive position

Chapter 7

Build the Structure

Build me straight, O worthy Master!
Staunch and strong, a goodly vessel.
                        —Henry Wadsworth Longfellow,
                        "The Building of the Ship," 1849

In Step 2, you created the strategy. The purpose of any strategy is to make tomorrow different from today. If you are satisfied with the present position and performance of your business, you have no need for a new strategy. All that is required is aligning everyone on a simple instruction: *keep on doing what you're doing now.* What triggers the need for a new strategy is an awareness, at minimum, that today is not good enough, that today is where you are but not where you aspire to be or desperately need to be. Sometimes this awareness is self-evident. It is clear that the business is floundering or even foundering. In this case, absent a strategy, change will come: things will get worse. Depending on how much worse, the business will fail either later or sooner.

Even if the leadership of the organization is aware that tomorrow needs to be different from today, Step 2 requires a deeper understanding of the present state of the business. This is acquired through the gathering of performance data and an 80/20 analysis. These two actions provide information that should drive divergent thinking. *Divergent thinking* is founded on understanding what's happening inside the box that represents the present state of the business but using that understanding to think outside the box to produce insights that will guide the creation of a strategy capable of making tomorrow different from today—in a good way, the way you want or need.

The strategy outlined in Step 2 must be based on updated assumptions and deep understanding of the situation of the business within the broader context of the environment in which the business operates. Step 3 takes these insights and uses them to articulate a vision of tomorrow, the desired and/or needed future state of the business. The vision takes the form of a structure or framework developed from the strategic objectives articulated in Step 2 and uses it to lay out the initiatives required to achieve the strategic objectives. Step 3 must deliver an executable strategy to realize the vision and mission of the business by implementing the right initiatives to achieve the right objectives. The ongoing test of whether these components of the vision and mission are, in fact, being achieved is the extent to which the business moves toward the financial goal set in Step 1. This movement is the key metric in assessing the success of the strategy.

Strategic Alignment and Cross-Functional Execution: The How

Step 2 laid out the need for strategic alignment (determining the focus of the company toward delivering profitable organic growth) and for the cross-functional execution of that focus. With regard to these two imperatives, Step 2 defined the *what*. Step 3 goes on to consider strategic alignment and cross-functional execution in broad rather than detailed terms of *how* these functions will run to achieve profitable share gain in the market by lowering operating costs and growing sales organically.

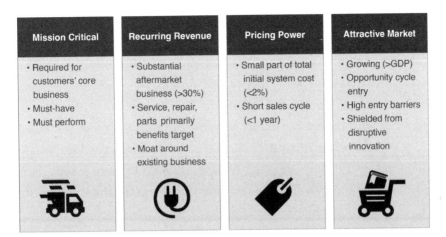

Mission Critical	Recurring Revenue	Pricing Power	Attractive Market
• Required for customers' core business • Must-have • Must perform	• Substantial aftermarket business (>30%) • Service, repair, parts primarily benefits target • Moat around existing business	• Small part of total initial system cost (<2%) • Short sales cycle (<1 year)	• Growing (>GDP) • Opportunity cycle entry • High entry barriers • Shielded from disruptive innovation

Figure 7-1   The Four Requirements for a Desirable M&A Target

When appropriate, Step 3 also takes the company beyond achieving profitable growth exclusively through the organic growth of sales. Leadership might also outline a plan for investing in further growth through geographic (territory) expansion, product line expansion, or both. Typically, this means making the strategic case for mergers and acquisitions (M&A). At this stage, M&A is only under consideration. Having defined promising areas for geographic and product line expansion, executives lay out the requirements for potential M&A targets by using four filters. These serve to narrow down prospects for an eventual initial offer of interest. Prospective M&A targets must meet criteria set by leadership in these four areas. Typical requirements for a viable M&A target must do the following (see Figure 7-1):

- **Produce mission-critical products or services:** The most attractive targets produce goods that are mandatory in the given industry or market rather than discretionary—needs to buy rather than want to buy.

- **Feature recurring revenue:** Look for acquisitions that offer opportunity for substantial aftermarket business. For many leaders, a target company's primary products are only as attractive as the aftermarket (accessories, installable upgrades, service, etc.) opportunities they open up. In companies I lead, "substantial aftermarket business" is considered north of 30 percent. A key source of recurring revenue is service, maintenance, repair, and parts sales. Finally, the acquisition target is made vastly more attractive if it is surrounded by a moat, which makes the cost of entry for competitors prohibitively expensive.

- **Offer pricing power:** The products or services of the target company should offer opportunities to exercise pricing power. Remember: all quads except Quad 1 (The Fort) either benefit from or absolutely require room to price up to profitability using 80/20 analysis. Products with short sales cycles (under one year) also provide pricing flexibility.

- **Be in an attractive market:** Common characteristics of such companies include evidence of ongoing growth with low cyclicality, availability for acquisition at an optimum stage in the business cycle, high entry barriers (to ward off newcomers), shielding from disruptive innovation.

Apply Divergent Thinking Followed by Convergent Thinking

The beauty of the 80/20 rule is that it is both clear and prescriptive. It will tell you what to do to make the numbers work so that the business can focus on The Fort and then allocate remaining resources to Quads 2 and 3 proportionately and either cut loose or price up customer/product combinations in Quad 4. What 80/20 will *not* do is tell you how to make all the moves to correctly apportion resources for optimum productivity.

Thinking is required. To be more precise, two methods of thinking are required: divergent and convergent. The most familiar form of divergent thinking is brainstorming: putting key people together in a room, giving them the insights produced by the situation analysis (the work of Steps 1 and 2), and asking them to generate as many ideas as possible on how to act on the insights to put the business on track to achieve its Step 1 goal. You want at this point a variety of ideas, options, and alternatives. Divergent thinking should be candid, freewheeling, and uncensored. The purpose is to surface all the possibilities, to evaluate the implications of the assessment, and then to inventory the strategic options available—or potentially available—to the business. Take a wide-angle view. In fact, stop at nothing. Be the most voracious pig at the trough. Consider options in as many of the following areas as possible:

- Adjacencies
- New market and product development
- Acquisitions and divestiture
- Network/footprint
- Making versus buying
- New capabilities
- Improving the core business
- Improving market attractiveness
- Improving competitive position

When the brainstorm dies down and options are exhausted, deem as complete the inventory of the possible that the team has produced. At this point, shift from divergent to convergent thinking (see Figure 7-2).

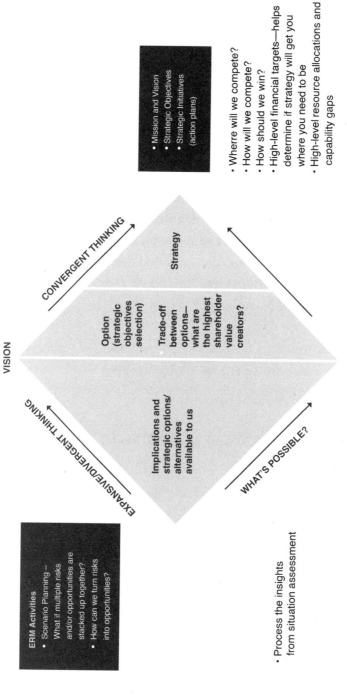

STRATEGIC FRAMEWORK

VISION

CONVERGENT THINKING

EXPANSIVE/DIVERGENT THINKING

Strategy

Option (strategic objectives selection)

Trade-off between options— what are the highest shareholder value creators?

Implications and strategic options/ alternatives available to us

WHAT'S POSSIBLE?

- Wherre will we compete?
- How will we compete?
- How should we win?
- High-level financial targets—helps determine if strategy will get you where you need to be
- High-level resource allocations and capability gaps

- Mission and Vision
- Strategic Objectives
- Strategic Initiatives (action plans)

ERM Activities
- Scenario Planning – What if multiple risks and/or opportunities are stacked up together?
- How can we turn risks into opportunities?

- Process the insights from situation assessment

Figure 7-2 Divergent/Convergent Thinking Cycle

From Panic to Profit

Interrogate each option with an eye toward discarding what will *not* work and, just as important, what is *not* imperative and *not* of the highest value. Set as your target winnowing the options to just two or three initiatives to prioritize as the objectives for the first full year of a strategic plan. If the group is persuaded that three initiatives are insufficient, consider five as the absolute maximum. These limits are not arbitrary. They are based on a consensus of executive experience, which teaches that exceeding five major initiatives in any one year is counterproductive in that it dilutes focus—the old jack of all trades and master of none syndrome.

Take what is now your shortlist of initiatives and prepare statements of strategic objectives and strategic initiatives. These statements are the first key deliverables of the convergent thinking process. Regard them as a preview of the actions needed to incrementally execute on a strategy that aims for the three- to five-year goal set in Step 1. The statements at this point should be reasonably complete regarding issues of *what, when, why, who,* and *where.* Fully articulating the *how* is the task of the next step, launch the action plan, which begins the implementation of the strategy.

The Three Questions to Answer Now

Simply put, the target of the convergent thinking phase is to define initiatives for the first full year of the strategic plan and to frame a strategy that adequately answers three questions:

- Where will we compete?
- How will we compete?
- Why will we win?

How do you know your answers to these questions are correct? Well, you don't know—at least not for certain and not yet. You won't know for sure until you have applied the two to five (three is ideal) strategic initiatives proposed in this step. That is why the execution of the strategy must be closely monitored and corrected along the way. In the first hundred days, you are positioning the company to earn the right to grow. If you have identified effective strategic priorities and implemented effective initiatives for executing them, you should see progress but not perfection. Progress is monitored and priorities and initiatives tweaked, modified, or changed accordingly. To begin with, however, executives must ensure that the priorities and their associated initiatives are integral with the company's three- to five-year mission, vision, and goal. Modifying or tuning the priorities and initiatives is guided by continuous monitoring and analysis of results with an eye toward further refinement of strategic objectives, scoping, rationale, and the evaluation of potential value at risk versus potential value creation.

While monitoring and evaluating performance, keep your eye on the prize, which not only includes the financial goal that has been set but also making certain that the chosen initiatives strengthen the core of the business, improve market attractiveness, and improve the competitive position of the business. The strategic framework aims at clarity, including a financial forecast based on crisply defined projections and with all initiatives defined by their projected P&L impact.

Sector and Product Line

Look back at Step 1, in which you set a three- or five-year *company-wide* financial goal. That was your *what*. Step 3 gets you through the *when*, *why*, *who*, and *where*, adding a framework view of the *how*. Carry the process deeper into the *how* by setting initial financial targets in *each sector* of the business and/or for *each product line*. This level of specificity aids in auditing the overall strategy by indicating what levers to pull as you begin to earn the right to grow.

Run your numbers for each sector and/or product line using the 80/20 processes described in Chapters 2–4. Identify gaps in resource allocation and capabilities. Determine what resources can be moved from Quads 2–4 to over-resource Quad 1 customers and products. (Hint: begin by moving resources from Quad 4.) Apply 80/20 at the sector/product line level to reevaluate the available trade-offs among the priorities and initiatives you have identified. Using your 80/20 results, focus or refocus on those most likely to produce the greatest profitability. The resulting subset of the "most likely" contains your key strategic objectives. Retain these and only these for the business/action plan.

Remember: the process at this point in Step 3 should be guided by convergent thinking. You are now lasering in on the best options, not spinning off possibilities. Filter out all but the highest-value opportunities by looking at their revenue and profit potential, affordability, and relative ease of execution in the context of the company's available core competencies and strategic assets. Ensure that the initiatives you have identified for the whole business are supported by each sector and/or product line. If not, filter your results even further from your initial cut until you are left with only the critical few strategic initiatives required to attain your objectives.

When you have narrowed your focus to key programs and projects, as well the actions, resources, organizational implications, and investments required to execute the strategic priorities, evaluate each within a quick-and-dirty long-term financial forecast covering the coming three to five years (depending on the time frame of your business plan). Any market expansion opportunities (including M&A) should be outlined and risks summarized.

At this point, you should have the framework of the business plan. It should clearly stake out the boundaries of the business as well as the strategic assets and core capabilities that will ensure a disciplined focus on the priorities. It should set out and explain relevant market and customer dynamics, the competitive landscape, the firm's positioning, and its sources of competitive advantage.

Deliverables

Step 3 can be deemed complete as soon as its suitcase of deliverables is fully packed. That suitcase carries a summary of *where* the business will compete, *what* capabilities are required to make it competitive, and *why* the business will win. In addition, this step provides a framework for *how* it will compete, the *how* being fleshed out and put into action in Step 4.

Packed into the Step 3 suitcase are the following:

- Mission and vision
- Prior year strategy overview
- Business environment assessment
- Strategic priorities summary, including strategic objectives, definition/scoping and rationale, and value potentially at risk/ potential value to be created
- Strategic priorities, consisting of two to five (three is a good target) strategic initiatives, likely including initiatives for strengthening the core of the business, improving market attractiveness, and improving competitive position
- Key programs/projects, actions, resources, organizational implications, and investments required to execute on the strategic priorities and initiatives

- Three- to five-year strategic financial forecast
- Draft of strategic initiative Gantt charts, including hypothesis, high-level timing, and resource requirements
- Market expansion opportunities (M&A), with risks summarized
- A concluding bullet list of critical success factors

But Remember, It's Still About Progress, Not Perfection

What is delivered in Step 3 is not complete. It is merely a bridge to Step 4: Launch the Action Plan, which is the business plan for the coming first full year. Step 3 is the framework for a strategic plan that builds on the strategic framework, with emphasis on all the *hows*. It is a more fully developed expression of the management team's vision for success. The dimensions by which the win is defined include customer, product, and operational effectiveness. Looking to the future, the framework answers this question: *What will be our position in the competitive marketplace?*

No vision of the future is perfect. The vision can be improved as it is reality-tested through time in the real world, but, within the brief compass of the first hundred days, the purpose of the vision is to get the organization moving in the right direction, toward Step 4 and increasingly well positioned to earn the right to grow. The first hundred days is always driven by a bias for action.

Even the fabled Sibyl of Cumae, whose temple cave can still be visited just outside of Naples (Italy, not Florida), never laid claim to perfection in predicting the future, although her fans tended to blame any failures on *human* misunderstanding of her divinely oracular pronouncements. Certainly, the work of a hundred days cannot promise sibylline infallibility, but the deliverables of Step 3 should provide a sturdy platform for the business plan—the action plan—that is the work of Step 4.

The action plan needs a *what*—based on the goal set in Step 1—followed by a *where*, defining the company's strategic customers (that is, its A customers) in the near and long term. Next comes the *how*, which applies the strategy to uniquely satisfying the company's A customers. The ultimate working test of the strategy is its success or failure in creating a sustainable competitive advantage for the next three to five years. The ultimate metric for this test is whether the strategy has carried the company to or beyond the goal defined in Step 1. Nothing is run on automatic pilot. Ever. You must set a goal, a target. As the quarters roll by, the strategy must be tuned and modified to keep it on track toward the target. The odds that it will emerge from the first hundred days perfect are vanishingly small. So, move on to Step 4 without glancing back.

Chapter 8

Launch the Action Plan

The readiness is all.

—Shakespeare, *Hamlet*, Act 5, Scene 2

The first hundred days culminate in Step 4, drafting and implementing an *action plan*, which defines the imperatives and tactics needed to execute the strategy drafted in Step 2 and segmented within the 80/20 structure laid out in Step 3.

This sounds like a lot, and it is, but although it is the end of the first hundred days, it is far from the end of the PGOS process. On November 10, 1942, during World War II, Winston Churchill delivered the traditional "Prime Minister's Address to the Lord Mayor's Banquet" at London's Mansion House. It followed the Second Battle of El Alamein (Egypt), in which British and Allied troops dealt German and Italian forces under the legendary Desert Fox, Field Marshal Erwin Rommel, a crushing blow. The victory came after a relentless series of humiliating British and Allied defeats and was thus a most welcome triumph. Churchill celebrated it in the speech, speaking at length about what he called a victory of the "men of British blood," but he closed with a carefully modulated appraisal: "This is not the end. It is not even the beginning of the end. But it is perhaps the end of the beginning."

And this is precisely the point to which Step 4 brings the business: the end of the beginning. Writers often speak of the "tyranny of the blank page." Defeating this tyranny by getting down on paper (or on the screen) the opening sentence, what untold generations of schoolteachers call "the topic sentence," or perhaps writing the lead paragraph, or drawing up a rough outline launches the memo, essay, blog, article, or book. Whether it is an online post or *War and Peace*, the end of the beginning launches the conversion of thought into action.

Step 4 is no less but also no more than this. It positions the business to earn the right to grow. It is, like the three steps that precede it, a work of progress (not perfection) toward reaching the goal set out in Step 1. Step 4 thrusts the company's strategy, however imperfect, into the real world, which will test it over the next year and, by testing it, reveal how to improve it so that it will reach or surpass the strategic goal by year three or year five, depending on the timeline of your business plan.

X-Matrix

As implemented through the PGOS, 80/20 analysis is a treasure map to profitable growth. Like any treasure map worthy of the name, it features a prominent *X* marking the spot. In this case, it is the sweet spot of efficient productivity in which the business is shaped and reshaped to focus its precious resources on the critical products, customers, markets, and initiatives. Called the *X-Matrix*, this map is a strategic planning tool originally used as part of Hoshin Kanri, a Japanese strategic management methodology. Like other modern Japanese management tools, the X-Matrix is a visually structured document designed to help companies align their strategic goals with executable plans and the metrics to monitor and evaluate their performance. The strategy and the business plan that follow from it are both inert schemes, mere theories, until they are implemented—*enacted.*

The business plan puts on record *what* you intend to accomplish, typically within three or five years. The action plan lays out *how* these things will be accomplished. A *plan* is an elaboration on an idea, but it is still an idea. *Action* is not an idea or a description of an idea. Action is an event that requires doers who do specific things at specific times. Once launched, a successful action plan connects the *ideas* envisioned in the business plan and expressed in the strategy to the *reality* of the business by assigning the *what*, *how*, and *who* that are needed to move ideas to acts.

- The *what* must be a clear definition of an action or set of actions and must enumerate the resources required to perform the action(s).

- The *how* consists of the strategic initiatives that were created as part of the strategic framework and strategy in Steps 2 and 3. These initiatives should be aimed at strengthening the core of the business, improving market attractiveness, improving competitive position, and/or decreasing costs to serve.

- The *who* identifies those with immediate leadership and immediate operational responsibility for implementing each aspect of the business plan. This is a critical dimension of the action plan because it is human beings, not abstractions, who make things happen. Operationally, the *who* has critical implications for personnel decisions and actions, such as internal promotions, transfers, and relocations as well as potential talent acquisition from outside the company.

For businesses looking to earn the right to grow—that is, to position themselves for a turnaround—the business plan and the action plan critical to implementing it should emphasize the following:

- Articulating and aligning on a mission statement, which defines how and where the company intends to win in the marketplace.

- Enumerating all major changes from the preceding year. Clearly, it is impossible to assess where you are going without knowing where you are, and, in turn, you cannot know where you are if you don't know where you were. Underscore the most impactful changes at the company as well significant changes in the marketplace, in technology, and in the competitive environment. Call out those changes that will make the greatest impact on the future of the business. To the degree possible at this early point in time, quantify the changes in terms of dollars, quantities, and percentages.

- Create a situation analysis. Apply a deliberately self-critical approach in presenting the salient facts about both the current and historical state of the business. Cast a bright and urgent light on where the company is winning and, even more important, where it is failing to win. In the first hundred days, the level of detail possible in the situation analysis will doubtless be constrained by time, but focusing on well-defined metrics will make it more meaningful. Consider, for example, breaking the business down by major product lines, and breaking down issues of growth and profitability by product. Your A products should be called out for special attention, as should B products capable of pricing up. You may also want to break the analysis down by state, region, or country. In the case of sales, the analysis may be segmented by channel. If technological innovation is important to your business, analyses of relevant trends in technology should be given special notice. If your business is significantly affected by government regulation (domestic and/or international), trends and impending legislation should be highlighted. For marketing, analyze markets by size, growth, product type, and customer. Do not neglect competitor market shares.

- With an eye toward the three- or five-year goal (Step 1), it is good practice to restate (or repeat the formulation of) the two to five high-priority objectives with respect to all the following parameters that apply:

- Customer segments to be penetrated

- New products/product lines to be developed

- Channels to access or develop capable of reaching the customer segments identified

- Operational effectiveness

- Data required

With the *what, how,* and *who* well-articulated, you are ready to apply the X-Matrix. This tool is a graphic aid to aligning strategies, goals, tactics, and measurements so that executives and managers across the enterprise can more effectively focus on strategic priorities. See Figure 8-1 for an X-Matrix template.

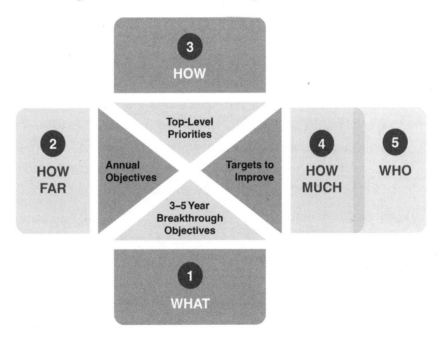

Figure 8-1 X-Matrix Template

An X-Matrix is read clockwise from the bottom, starting with the South sector and moving up and to the left (West), thence to the top (North), and down and to the right (East). In creating the X-Matrix, unit or segment leaders may focus on the areas of their immediate responsibility, but all segments of the business must be assembled in the final matrix.

- The South is the *what*, which means that the focus is on the goal set in Step 1 and the objectives that must be achieved to get to that goal, which may be labeled the three- or five-year breakthrough goal. Because we are looking to bring the business plan to life, the objectives are largely defined financially in terms of EBITDA (earnings before interest, taxes, depreciation, and amortization); margins; and issues of organic or inorganic growth.

- The West, which may be labeled *how far*, still concerns the *what* but zeros in on the short-term objectives (we can call them *milestones*) that must be achieved on an annual basis to ensure that the long-term breakthrough goal is attained. The questions this sector of the matrix answers are *How far* have we come? and *How far* do we have yet to go? The West is a monitoring, feedback, and adjustment direction, which reveals the need and magnitude of adjustments required to course-correct in the journey toward the breakthrough goal.

- The North summarizes the top strategic priorities and the accompanying initiatives required to carry out the mission, realize the vision, execute the strategic objectives, and attain the long-term breakthrough goal. The top strategic priorities should be subject to quarterly evaluation/reevaluation in terms of both value at risk and value creation potential. In Step 4, the priorities must be justified in terms of their focus, key projects, resources required, investments required, as well risks and rewards.

148

- The East consists of targets to improve (TTIs—leading indicators) and key performance indicators (KPIs—lagging indicators). This is another sector dedicated to monitoring and feedback with the objective of continuous improvement, again in pursuit of the breakthrough goal. The work here is focused on determining how to most meaningfully track priorities and objectives. The tracking metrics are reviewed during regular monthly business reviews. The idea is to determine how much is being achieved, how much more could be achieved, and how much more should be achieved. The answers to the "how much" have implications for the *who*: the assignment of persons responsible for leading each aspect of the action plan. Accountability is assigned on the assumption that nothing gets done without an individual held accountable for doing it. Names are named!

Another aspect of the action plan in the East is called *cascading*. Individual business units may be assigned not only a *priority* in the action plan but also the *autonomy* to create or improve the unit's processes that are related to achieving the TTIs. In other words, accountability and autonomy may be cascaded down to individual business units. Such cascading should be specified in Step 4 as part of the organizational process of earning the right to grow. The TTIs—the targets—themselves do not change, just the scope of responsibility and accountability for executing them within the business unit.

Scope of the Step 4 Action Plan

Within the first hundred days, the business plan (Step 3) is an aspirational work-in-progress, but it emerges at the conclusion of the step as ready for a place in the action plan (Step 4) that will launch it into the real world. Think in terms of agile software development, which formally debuted at the beginning of the twenty-first century as a way to accelerate software development through an iterative and incremental approach. The idea was to bring out a workable beta product not with the intention of perfection but of continuous improvement in response to real-world use case scenarios. The product of an urgent process, the action plan is at best a beta iteration, but it is sufficiently advanced to define key tactics and the efforts required to execute that other work-in-progress, the business plan.

The action plan stipulates the principal actions required to advance the business toward the breakthrough goal. That is, the beta-deliverable action plan is more granular than an alpha-level iteration because it breaks down high-level elements into multiple specific tasks. How do you go from alpha to beta? The answer is obvious: *Always think in terms of* actions.

The X-Matrix helps the team to deliver an action plan that aligns executives and managers, putting them in position to launch the strategy. Prior to delivery, evaluate the action plan to ensure that it satisfies the items in this checklist:

- **Sufficiently recaps the goal defined in the business plan:** A hundred days may seem like a brief span in which to plot out and ignite a business transformation, but it is a full business quarter. Don't assume that everyone focused on Step 4 will have the content and achievements of Steps 1–3 at the top of mind by the time they approach Step 4. Recap Steps–3 to reinforce the context for the actions that must be defined in Step 4. Reiterate the breakthrough goal and the objectives toward that goal.

- **Sufficiently recaps the objectives defined in the business plan:** Having recapped the financial goal, Step 4 should inventory the objectives, milestones, and any other intermediate deliverables toward that goal.

- **Sufficiently defines and lays out the action steps (the projects) needed to achieve each objective outlined in the business plan:** Action steps are sometimes called *projects*. Whatever you call them, they are a set of related tasks (action items) that must be executed to produce each objective. It will not be possible to lay out all objectives in the first hundred days because additional objectives will doubtless emerge over the first full year and throughout the span of the business plan. By the same token, some objectives will be substantially modified or dropped entirely. This is the essence of agile development.

- **Clearly identifies and prioritizes all necessary action items:** As noted, action steps (projects) are made up of a sequence of subtasks called *action items*. These should be broken out and prioritized in the action plan, because they constitute a set of instructions for carrying out each action step.

- **Defines roles and responsibilities:** Having defined, divided, and subdivided the work required to execute the action plan, complete the East quadrant of the X-Matrix by designating the *who*. An effective action plan at this stage will not be complete, but assigning ownership of each enumerated action step (project) is important because action requires people (doers of the action), including at least one person accountable for the results of the action. To the extent possible, all necessary tasks should be assigned by the end of the first hundred days. Of course, roles and responsibilities will evolve and change during the three or five years to which the business plan applies.

- **Allocates resources:** Step 4 roughs out the allocation of management resources to the action steps included in the action plan. The East quadrant of the X-Matrix not only assigns management personnel to tasks but also, as needed, specifies the allocation of any additional resources required for each action step. This may include funding, equipment, physical plant, materials, advanced computing time, outside consultants, workspace, special certifications or licenses, and so on. As deemed necessary in the action plan, cascading empowers individual business units to create or improve their own processes to better carry out the action steps within the unit's purview. Ultimately, however, all resource allocations must be made within the context of the business plan to avoid suboptimization, which is a prime cause of *muda* (waste).

- **Allocates time:** Each action step and each action item requires time. To the extent possible within the span allotted for Step 4, create a timeline that breaks down action steps into action items. Provide reasonable deadlines for each item and step.

- **Applies the SMART standard to objectives:** The action plan requires close monitoring of performance (see "Do-Check-Act" section that follows) and the delivery of continuous feedback. It is a mistake to rely on subjective assessments, gut feelings, and hunches in assessing progress toward goals. In 1911, the pioneering efficiency expert Frederick Taylor stressed the importance of measuring what you monitor and using the resulting empirical data to find the best ways to run each production process. This was the cornerstone of his concept of "scientific management." Today, this quantified, objective approach is often identified by the acronym SMART: *specific, measurable, assignable, realistic*, and *time-related*. All action steps and items should embody these qualities, and their progress should be evaluated according to them. Evaluate each goal and deliverable in SMART terms so that you can be assured of accurately evaluating progress toward your business goals.

Sequencing Action Items

Usually, there is an optimal or even mandatory sequence in which action items are to be performed. Setting out action items requires more than a random list. The action plan should specify which items depend on completing other items first. By identifying these dependencies, a clear *when* takes its place beside the *what*.

Even when sequencing according to dependency is not absolutely mandatory, doing so invariably increases efficiency, allows for coordination of effort within a team and among teams, and generally saves time and lowers costs. Waste—as the Japanese use in the "Toyota Way," *muda*—is the enemy of the lean efficiencies that contribute mightily to the competitive edge a business enjoys.

The action plan created in Step 4 will almost certainly benefit from including a graphical timeline of action steps and the action items within each step. Graphical representation of actions through time not only simplifies project management but also enforces accountability, which is essential to efficiency. Again, manage expectations, as it will not be possible to anticipate, let alone include, every detail in an action plan drawn up in the first one hundred days.

SMART Objectives

As mentioned, SMART objectives are *specific, measurable, assignable, realistic,* and *time-related*. Every objective and goal enumerated in the action plan should satisfy the SMART requirement. If an objective cannot be described in these five dimensions, it should be revised until it can be. After all, these are the critical dimensions of the real world. If an objective cannot be evaluated against this scale, it will be impossible to track and assess progress toward

(continued)

(continued)

execution and the impact of implementation. Dumb objectives do not necessarily have to be discarded. They must, however, be modified until they meet the SMART criteria. So, ask and answer these questions:

- **Is the objective specific?** Why is the goal important? Who must be involved in achieving it? What additional resources will be required?
- **Is the objective measurable?** It is widely believed but not absolutely certain that the great Peter Drucker actually said, "What gets measured gets done." But I do hope he said it, because the statement is worthy of him and certainly needs to be said as well as acted on. Everyone involved in executing the action plan must know where they are going and how far they have gone. As Yogi Berra most definitely said, "If you don't know where you are going, you might wind up someplace else."
- **Is the objective assignable?** Can the action items and action steps necessary to achieving the objective in question be assigned to managers and other personnel capable of executing them? In other words, does the business have personnel who can do (and who have the bandwidth for) what needs to be done? If not, can such people be found outside the company?
- **Is the objective realistic?** Stretching toward a difficult objective or goal is healthy but ask, Is this particular objective feasible. Don't set people up for failure. Assess feasibility.
- **Is the objective time-related?** Leave no loose ends. Create timelines terminating in deadlines. Absent either of these, it is impossible to reliably coordinate multiple tasks.

From Panic to Profit

Do-Check-Act

Urgency is a powerful motivator. Urgency is the engine that drives the first hundred days. When you are endeavoring to earn the right to grow, you literally cannot afford to wait for perfection. The purpose of Step 4 is to create an action plan that produces rational decisions capable of advancing the business forward into the real world. Once the molecules are in motion outside of a test tube and in the arena of real life, they will bounce around, bounce off each other, combine, and interact. Continuously monitoring the ongoing results of this ferment will tell you how to further shape and amend the action plan, the business plan, and the strategy behind both. Whatever else launching the action plan *might* produce, it *will* generate data, and that is the substance required for making progress toward your goal.

Once launched, activate a Do-Check-Act process, which will help to ensure abundant and accurate feedback as the team monitors the unfolding progress of the action plan:

- **Do:** Execute the plan and collect data on results. Implement data-based modifications, course corrections, and improvements.

- **Check:** Evaluate the results produced by the modifications, course corrections, and improvements. Assess the execution of the plan. Verify the effectiveness of your changes, and continuously evaluate the timeliness for realizing the benefit of those changes. Do not narrowly search for confirmation, but investigate root causes. Learn as well from failure. It will instruct you in what necessary changes to make. Most important, continuously strive to improve the team's problem-solving skills. What worked? What did not work? And why?

- **Act:** Based on doing and checking, decide on the next steps in executing the business plan with an eye toward continuous improvement.

Launch the Action Plan

Try, Try Again

The action plan has two purposes:

- **Number one:** to convert the business plan from potential energy into kinetic energy
- **Number two:** to ensure that the conversion is feasible in the present but continuously modifiable to accommodate changing aspects of the real world

Do-Check-Act will be a leading process throughout the coming full year and for the entire three- to five-year course of the long-term business plan. The work of the first hundred days is bound to change. Iterate, iterate, iterate is just another way of saying try again, always bearing in mind that if you want tomorrow to be different from today, do something different—today.

After the First Hundred Days

Chapter 9

Exercise Your Right to Grow

Speech that leads not to action, still more that hinders it, is a nuisance on the earth.

—Thomas Carlyle, letter to his future wife,
November 4, 1825

The first hundred days earns the business the right to grow. The first full year of the business plan's implementation is all about continuous improvement driven by simplification riding the rails of 80/20 (see the 80/20 tools in Chapters 2–4). You simplify what can, should, and must be simplified, which will earn you the right and capacity to grow what can, should, and must be grown.

Managing Real Time

Exercising the business's right to grow begins when the deliverables of the first hundred days are implemented in the first full year of the new business plan (see Figure 9-1).

The process must now proceed relentlessly in real time. The strategic management process is dynamic and meted out on pace each quarter and in sync with monthly business reviews. The rhythm is a driving beat throughout the first full year following the first hundred days and is sustained for the full course of the three- or five-year business plan.

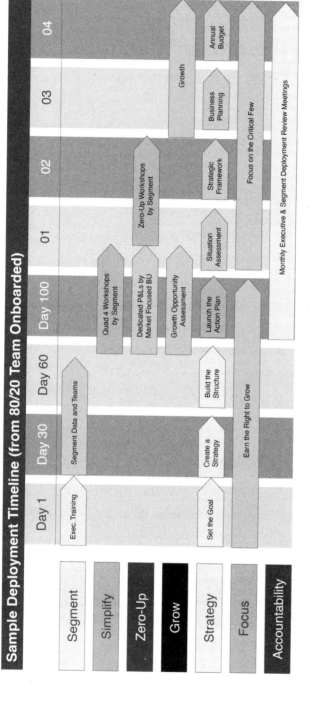

Figure 9-1 First Hundred Days Timeline

Within the first hundred days, the process of earning the right to grow was carried out in four steps:

1. Setting the goal
2. Framing the strategy
3. Building the structure
4. Launching the action plan

Steps 3 and 4 are intensively guided by 80/20 simplification.

- Quad 4 customer/product combinations are priced up or out using the tools and processes in Chapters 2–4.
- Dedicated profit and losses (P&Ls) are created within market-focused business units.
- A comprehensive assessment of growth opportunities is made.

These three processes carry Step 3 into the Step 4 action plan. They are, in turn, the transitional link to the first quarter of the first full year of the new business plan.

The Strategic Management Process in Q1 and Q2

Q1 of this first year initiates an 80/20 focus on "the critical few"—that roughly 20 percent of product/customer combinations, investments, and initiatives that drive 80 percent of revenue. This focus continues throughout the entire first year of the new business plan and, indeed, drives the strategy throughout the entire duration of the plan as it advances toward the financial goal set at the very beginning of the first hundred days.

During Q1 of Year 1, the management team performs a comprehensive situation assessment, which is the central feature of the quarterly report. Zero-up activity, perhaps in the form of workshops dedicated by segment, might begin in Q1 and carry over into Q2, in which the focus is on the performance and improvement of the strategic framework.

The strategic management process during Year 1's Q2 is focused on the performance assessment and improvement of the strategic framework. In addition to the ongoing 80/20 focus on the critical few, the segment-focused zero-up workshops, begun in Q1, continue to advance and refine 80/20 efforts to establish or reestablish the business with precisely the level of resources necessary to optimally serve the critical few. The purpose of this work is to reduce or eliminate the trivial many and the disproportionate volume of resources squandered on serving low-performing customers and low-margin or no-margin products.

Zero-up is all about deploying the most effective strategy to address and correct the natural imbalance between outlays and income. The problem it seeks to solve is simple yet pernicious: the more resources you devote to B customers and B products, the more destructive the imbalance becomes. Contrary to what common sense (often a most destructive bias) might tell you, throwing more resources at underperforming customers, products, and entire segments will *not* rehabilitate them. Think lipstick on a pig, polish on a turd. Diversion of resources to low-margin and no-margin customers and products does nothing more or less than squander effort and assets. Even worse, it compromises and dilutes the company's ability to serve high-performing customers. The fact that just 20 percent of input produces 80 percent of results tells us that the 20 percent is overperforming. Wonderful! But the business that fails to overperform in serving the 20 percent of its customers who produce 80 percent of its net sales will lose those overperforming A customers along with the ability to create or attract new A-level overperformers. It is overperformance on the part of the business that creates and attracts customers who consistently overperform.

Q2 of Year 1 is really just part of the beginning of the journey toward the goal set in Step 1 of the first hundred days. If the business is not overfocused on Quad 1 to the point of optimizing performance, you urgently need to fix it. Unfortunately, although the urgency is pressing, there is no quick fix for refocusing a misfiring business on Quad 1.

Tough break. Nevertheless, the faster the team does focus or refocus energy and resources on top-performing customers and products, the better the company's chances of earning the right to grow. Your business might need to scrap everything and start from scratch. If so, segmenting is critical because only the smallest businesses can find it even remotely feasible, let alone practical, to do a hard reboot.

So, emulate a small business by focusing on one segment at a time, proceeding segment-by-segment and P&L by P&L. Identify and target one underperforming segment of the business and treat it as if it were the whole business. Zero-up that segment as described in Chapter 4 to discover the minimum resources and costs required to run it and it alone. This will reveal the true costs of complexity while also unmasking areas in which costs can be reduced or even removed. Budget this segment not for five years or three years or even the coming year, but for the coming month only (see "The Zero-up Process in a Nutshell").

The Zero-Up Process in a Nutshell

Zero-up has one goal and one goal only. It is to help you to establish or reestablish the business with the level of resources necessary to optimally serve the critical few. Achieving this goal means reducing or eliminating the trivial many and the disproportionate volume of resources it takes to serve low-performing customers and low-margin or no-margin products. In business, imbalance between outlays and income ranges from suboptimal to downright destructive. The more resources you devote to B customers

(continued)

(continued)

and B products, the more destructive the imbalance. Diversion of resources to low-margin and no-margin customers and products squanders effort and assets. Even worse, it compromises the company's capacity to serve high-performing customers. Fail to overperform for the 20 percent of your customers who produce 80 percent of your net sales, and you will lose them along with the ability to create or attract new A customers (see Figure 9-2).

There is no quick fix for a business incapable of converting B customers into A customers. But the faster you productively refocus energy and resources on top-performing customers and products, the better your chances of turning the company around. Few businesses can afford to scrap everything and start from scratch. But a from-scratch turnaround can be made segment by segment. Prioritize one underperforming segment of the business and, in effect, start from scratch to balance it. Zero-up in that segment to discover the minimum resources and costs required to run it minimally. This reveals the hidden costs of complexity while also exposing areas in which costs can be reduced or even removed. Budget for the coming month. Start with zero and add to it the individual costs of what is needed for the month. Take the resulting total of these outlays and compare it to the income from the month. If outlays exceed income, you have a choice. Subtract from your outlays or add to your income or do both. Next month, start from zero again, rinse, and repeat.

Zeroing up is harsh, but working a month at a time, starting from scratch each month on a given segment, is doable and will enable you to identify the assumptions that drive the segment. The needs are the high priority. The wants are optional, at least more or less. If it proves impossible to satisfy needs without incurring loss, the segment is beyond saving. Drop it.

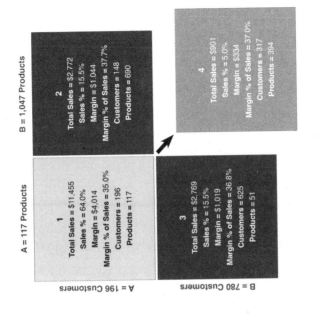

Inputs — Benefits of Simplification

- Identify profitable segments of business that are desirable to grow
- Activities driving need for people
- Required for Success: Compelling vision for how eliminating Quad 4 will improve business performance

Execution — Pivot to Growth

- Leadership team aligns on Quads 1–3 resourcing & pro-forma P&L
- Identifies ~20–25% of overhead resources supporting Quad 4
- Required for Success: Active, informed senior leadership engagement

Outputs — 80/20 Strategic Plan

- Multiyear customer focused strategy for growth, profitability
- Self-fund resources required for growth initiatives
- Required for Success: Executive sponsorship to drive resourcing

Figure 9-2   Zero-Up in a Nutshell

You will need to repeat this zero-up process each month for each targeted segment month after month. There is no zero-up shortcut. It is not feasible to attempt to create a zero-base budget for the next three or five years any more than you can create, say, a family budget for that length of time. There are too many variables and, more to the point, too many variables beyond anyone's ability to predict adequately. What the segment-by-segment, month-by-month zero-up will accomplish, however, is to make it easier to identify the assumptions that drive the segment. It will allow the management team to separate *needs* from *wants*. The imperative is to prioritize the identified *needs* of the business, focus precious resources on them, and then allocate whatever is left over to the highest-performing *wants*. Those *wants* that cannot be adequately served, even by pricing up, must be dropped. By the same token, if the needs of a segment prove impossible to satisfy without incurring loss, the entire segment must be jettisoned.

The Strategic Management Process in Q3 and Q4

The concluding days of the first hundred days set the stage for zeroing-up with a focus on Quad 4 and creating dedicated P&Ls by market-focused business units. This concluding portion of the first hundred days is also devoted to assessing opportunities for growth. Having targeted segments for zero-up simplification in the first two quarters, it is on the growth opportunities that the management team focuses during Q3 and Q4. Growth drives review and tweaking of the business plan in Q3 and is enshrined in the annual budget that is the object of review and revision in Q4.

Business planning (Q3) and the coming year's annual budget (Q4) bring together the 80/20 simplification of Q1 and Q2 to create an increasingly productive focus on the critical few, which is the imperative for profitable growth. Ideally, the annual budget drawn up in Q4 is for a company that has earned its right to grow and is now executing a strategy of growth.

Cycle and Flywheel

Segment, simplify, zero-up, grow—you can look at this as a sequence or, even more meaningfully, as a cycle. Cycles can be bad or good. *Vicious* cycles, in which the response to one difficulty or crisis creates new problems, are bad, whereas *virtuous* cycles are good. Done right, segment, simplify, zero-up, grow is a virtuous cycle because it creates a flywheel effect (see Figure 9-3). As hard as the work of the first hundred days and then the first year of the new business plan is, it all pays off in a flywheel that gains momentum and, overcoming the inertia by which a body at rest tends to remain at rest, enters the phase of the inertial state in which a body in motion tends to remain in motion. We are not talking about perpetual motion (energy out of nothing), but a process of continuous real-time adjustment, tweaking, tuning, and sometimes taking such drastic action as jettisoning product lines and even entire segments or innovating in identified growth areas. But know this: once you push, pull, and shove 80/20 your way, the business tends to roll faster and faster.

The first move is to *segment* the business based on customer and product data (Chapter 3) to identify the top-performing customer/product combinations in the business and thus the most profitable P&Ls within the business. These combinations are elevated to Quad 1, the 20 percent that produce 80 percent of revenue and that cry out to be overserved. To further increase the efficiency with which these business units might be served, separate unlike businesses.

Having identified the A customers, A products, and A business units on the one hand and the lowest-performing B customers,

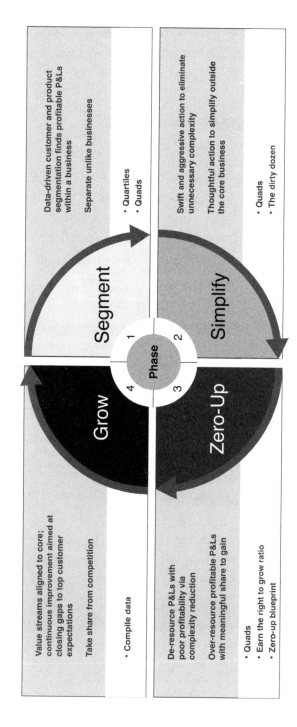

Figure 9-3 The Four-Phase 80/20 Cycle: Basis for a Flywheel

From Panic to Profit

products, and business units on the other, aggressively *simplify* the business. Speed is of the essence. Each underperforming stockkeeping unit (SKU) is a potential aneurysm ready to bleed you. Take action to stop the hemorrhage of wasted service and squandered cash before it starts. Price up, simplify sales channels, engage the underperformers minimally by stressing online sales and other forms of self-service. Jettison products and even entire segments that cannot be made profitable. Then rejoice in the consequent exodus of those customers who are throttling your business. Focus on the core but also apply thoughtful action beyond The Fort. Think before you banish products and customers. Realize profit wherever it might lurk. Apply the full panoply of the dirty dozen to rehabilitate underperformers (Chapter 3).

Amplify the simplification of the business by zeroing-up, as outlined in the discussion of Q3 and Q4 activity. De-resource P&Ls in which the P is either flagging or downright dead. The resulting reduction in complexity will go a long way toward lowering costs, thereby restoring profitability to at least some faltering customer/ product combinations. Move the resources to Quad 1 to juice the most profitable P&Ls by over-resourcing the A-customer base. Use the right to grow ratios to help guide you (Chapter 4).

Segment, simplify, zero-up: *Now* you have earned the right to do some growing, so *grow*. Ensure that value streams are aligned to the core of the business. Relentlessly practice continuous improvement not merely to meet A-customer expectations but to exceed them. Do not settle for *customer satisfaction*. Target and create *customer delight*, which will win *customer loyalty*. When your business becomes the go-to in one category and market and location after another, you will start to take market share from your competitors. It is not enough to do well. You need to do *really* well by crushing the competition. That is the energy that transforms this four-phase cycle into a flywheel sufficient to drive profitable growth.

Celebrate the Wins, Cultivate the Fear

Progress, not perfection: Celebrate the progress you are making toward the goal set five quarters ago, back in Step 1 of the first hundred days. But don't relax and don't relent. You could lose it, lose all of it. So, let that fear drive continued vigilance, a deep reverence for data, and a desire to improve on a continuous basis.

Why do we love underdog stories? Why flash a thumbs up to David but flip the bird to Goliath? Because the underdogs and the Davids are dynamic, unburdened by dead weight, doing more with less, and the incumbents are fat, self-satisfied, complacent, and uninterested in improvement. They might actually remain incumbent for a long time, but—honestly—they deserve to fail and something inside each of us is eager to see them go down.

So, eyes on the prize, eyes wide awake, eyes wide with fear—and also with excitement. It feels good to win, but if you want to keep feeling that way, you must win and win again and again. Reject the complacency of incumbency. It is a loser and therefore something you need to be afraid of.

Chapter 10

Tune the Critical Focus

We take the hamburger business more seriously than anyone else.
—Ray Kroc

Born in 1902, Ray Kroc dropped out of high school to drive an ambulance on the Western Front in World War I, after which he knocked around as a dance band musician before finding a straight job as sales manager for the Lily-Tulip Paper Cup and Plate Company. From here, he became a traveling salesman hawking milkshake-mixing machines. One day in 1954, one of his milkshake-machine customers, the McDonald Brothers of San Bernardino, California, suddenly placed orders for an inordinate number of mixers. Pleased by the windfall, Kroc nevertheless decided to look this particular gift horse in the mouth. He paid a call on the McDonald boys and discovered that their San Berdoo burger joint was drawing quite a crowd. Kroc sampled their product and thought it was the best burger he'd ever had. Even more impressive, however, was the speed with which it had been prepared.

He talked to the boys, who, it turned out, were justifiably proud to show off their little business. They employed assembly-line-like techniques to prepare burgers with a consistent level of taste and quality in a spic-and-span shop. Their employees were almost exclusively low-paid but well-trained high-school-age workers. Kroc's first impression was that this drive-in was pure suburban Americana.

But as he gave the operation more thought, he realized that the McDonalds were missing the point. They emulated an assembly line in everything but scale. The combination of division of labor among low-paid, unskilled—but carefully trained—workers, the regimented routinization of tasks, and adherence to impeccable standards of cleanliness produced a low-priced, high-quality, 100 percent dependable product that appealed to the guys' suburban clientele. And when Kroc told them they should open up more restaurants—a whole lot of them—they told him they had franchised a few identical restaurants in the area—but they had no desire to go beyond this. Kroc kept pressing, proposing a mammoth scheme to scale up through intensive franchising. He more-or-less dragged the brothers along and, in 1955, established the McDonalds Corporation, opening a restaurant in the Chicago suburb of Des Plaines.

The rest, as they say, is history. McDonald's became a fast-food juggernaut as well as a national and—soon—global real estate empire. While other fast-food players tried to muscle in, Mickey D's remained by far the top incumbent for decades. By the end of the twentieth century, its restaurants had sold more than 65 billion burgers through some ten thousand restaurants.

If the chain's customers were fat and happy, McDonald's leadership was even fatter and happier. The business model, though huge, was simple. McDonald's restaurants allowed some variations but were basically iterations of the same structure. McDonald's menu—for many years—was a model of simplification. There were a few variations on the familiar hamburger, fries, and soft drink combination, but nothing truly outside the formula that had worked for years.

And then came a decline, as other fast-food restaurants scaled up, offered some novelty, offered other foods, and offered different looks. No business can maintain the status quo forever. One way or another, a business must profitably grow or shrink—either profitably or unprofitably. It can continue to get bigger, but if it remains static, growth in mere size and product offerings will only pull it down. At last, in 2014, the downward slide could no longer be ignored.

As sales diminished, stock valuations followed the slide. The CEO at the time, Don Thompson, believed he knew what was wrong. In recent years, as competitors began eating McDonald's lunch, so to say, the chain tried adding variety to its menu. And they added and added some more. Thompson believed that the menu had become too complicated, causing customer paralysis at the drive-up window. It took a while for the full Mickey D C-suite to buy into what Vilfredo Pareto had known since the late nineteenth century—that about 80 percent of effort and investment is frittered away on the trivial many and only 20 percent productively serves the critical few.

So, at long last, leadership aligned on an effort to simplify McDonald's hundred-plus-item menu, mercilessly dropping five Extra Value Meals and eight other items, including variations on the Quarter Pounder with Cheese, Premium Chicken sandwich, and Snack Wrap. McDonald's refocused on its high-performing products, the roughly 20 percent of meal offerings that most customers wanted most of the time. Moreover, because customers were no longer bewildered by an excess of choice, order lines moved much faster through the drive-up, delivering what McDonald's customers wanted more than anything else from their fast-food experience, which is to say *fast* food.

Your Most Powerful Tool

As McDonald's discovered, simplification is the most powerful tool in the 80/20 toolkit. By segmenting the business, you can focus it on what works and discard or modify what does not work. Common sense might seem to argue against this. McDonald's is a fast-food restaurant, so why not make it *the* fast-food restaurant that offers the greatest array of choices? We hold this truth to be self-evident, that choice is a great thing. And if a little choice is good, a lot of choice must be better. It's just plain good common sense!

But when McDonald's leadership looked at the data—what customers were actually buying, and what customers actually said—they reluctantly reached a different conclusion. Number one, most customers bought hamburgers (or cheeseburgers) and fries and mostly passed up the alternatives offered. (*Salads! Are you frickin' kidding me?*) Number two, McDonald's is a fast-food restaurant, but the hundred-item menu was slowing everything down. Diners seeking to enjoy a leisurely dinner at wait-list reservations-only Chez Chic are willing to wait. Those seeking *fast* food, however, will tolerate no delay and go instead to the Burger King across the street from the McDonald's bloated line-up and line.

In the 1933 Marx Brothers movie *Duck Soup*, Chico asks, "Who ya gonna believe, me or your own lyin' eyes?" Today, the shade of Vilfredo Pareto asks us, "Who ya gonna believe, your own prejudiced assumptions, or the numbers revealed by segmenting your business to separate the profitable from the unprofitable P&Ls?"

Simplification is the 80/20 process that enables you to focus your business on the critical few through segmentation. In the first hundred days, you did a relatively quick-and-dirty version of segmentation and used it primarily to simplify the underperforming B-customer/ B-product combinations in Quad 4. The least profitable segment of your business is not all that hard to identify. You can therefore be reasonably confident about your urgent first hundred days calculations and the decisions made from them concerning this saddest of all quads. But the first full year of the business plan that was hatched in the first hundred days is an opportunity to further tune the focus on the critical few based on ever-refreshed data acquired in real time.

If you were Michelangelo chiseling out his *David*, you would have the benefit of continuous feedback from your hands and eyes as the sculpture took shape. The action of the chisel in your hand would be the only input affecting the output embodied in the marble. This is an advantage the sculptor enjoys over the leaders of a business, who must contend with multiple inputs from multiple sources through long spans of time. Although the sculptor might aim for perfection, those running a business can strive toward their financial goal through a continuously evolving action plan shaped not by the impact of a chisel guided by a single hand but of multiple inputs from multiple sources within the context of markets and business environments formed and deformed by innumerable and often quite unpredictable forces. The most you can hope for is progress, not perfection—but it is progress nevertheless marked by increasing accuracy that yields profitable growth.

The Butterfly Effect Means Your Business Plan Will Never Be Perfect. Deal with It.

Edward Lorenz was an MIT professor and meteorologist who, in 1972, gave a presentation at a meeting of the American Association for the Advancement of Science he called "Predictability: Does the Flap of a Butterfly's Wings in Brazil Set Off a Tornado in Texas?"

Working in the days long before the advent of artificial intelligence, Lorenz was developing a digital algorithm to analyze the effect of atmospheric phenomena on weather so that he could better predict weather conditions in a given place at a given time. He tested the first iteration of his program by applying it to historical weather data. This enabled him to evaluate the accuracy of the predictions the program produced, comparing the prediction to the known historical outcome. His software predicted sunshine in a certain location on a certain day. Great! But then he looked at what had actually happened in that place and on that day.

(continued)

And it was rain, lots and lots of rain.

As a scientist, Lorenz understood that failure teaches as much as success. He dug back through his work in search of a wrong turn. But as far as he could make out, the software had done everything right. Confirmation is always comforting, but a scientist looks even harder for exception, which is typically far more useful. After much review, he finally recognized a possibly significant variable. Back in 1972, computing power and digital memory were trivial in comparison to what we take for granted today. This being the case, Lorenz sought to save precious bytes and processing time by performing his calculations only to the thousandth decimal place, which seemed to him both economical and more than sufficient.

But, he asked himself, *What if it wasn't?* What if the calculations were simply too gross to reveal the truth?

So, he tried calculating the same data to the ten thousandth decimal place and got the same erroneous result. Undeterred, he reran the algorithm to the hundred thousandth decimal place. With this adjustment, the forecast came up rain.

A humble weather scientist, Lorenz suddenly found himself the pioneer of a new field: chaos theory. Having developed a mathematical model to track how air moved around in the global atmosphere, he discovered that the most minute differences in the data he put into his algorithm—the difference between rounding to the thousandth decimal place versus the hundred thousandth—yielded enormously different weather forecasts. This prompted the conclusion that within the *apparent* randomness of large dynamic systems such as global atmospheric conditions, minute differences in the initial inputs can trigger major unexpected changes later in time and

(continued)

From Panic to Profit

(continued)

even at downstream locations quite remote from those inputs. He called this phenomenon a "sensitive dependence on initial conditions," but it has come to be known as the Butterfly Effect, which is dramatic shorthand for the fact that some seemingly insignificant input like the flapping of a butterfly's wings in Brazil can affect the trajectory of something as momentous, say, as a tornado in Texas.

Lorenz discovered that his forecasting calculations were insufficiently granular, so gross, in fact, that they missed the most critical cause-and-effect relationships altogether. For business leaders, the first hundred days of an effort to earn the right to grow will yield an abundance of data that can be used to guide initial initiatives of segmentation and simplification. But, given the urgency of a company in need of a turnaround and the limitations of short-term data, the numbers will likely be too gross to create optimal predictive guidance. Only repeated iterations of the four-phase cycle of segment, simplify, zero-up, and grow throughout the first full year of the deployment of a new business plan will enable executives to tune the focus on the critical few more precisely and productively. As the iterations are repeated throughout the full span of the business plan—typically three to five years—the focus will become sharper and sharper, the predictions more and more accurate, and the adjustments more and more effective in driving profitable growth. Will you eventually find perfection? No. But you will be getting warmer all the time.

To productively simplify complexity in the areas most important to the business, you will almost certainly need to reduce the number of products or models in a product line along with the number of markets and types of customers your sales organization dedicates its resources to reaching and serving. As Tim Nelson and Jim McGee wrote in their *Thinking Inside the Box: Discover the Exceptional Business Inside Your Organization,* "Major operational streamlining breakthroughs typically occur only after going through the line simplification process" (WCG Press 2013, p. 53).

Expect to encounter resistance. Most folks in business have been taught to fight tooth and nail for every single customer and every single order. Every customer is a good customer and every order is a good order, they say. An admirable attitude—unless the customer or the product or both are costing the business cash with each and every sale. There are also, for lack of a better term, "political" considerations. Top managers, sales chiefs, or innovators might have vested interests in this product or that customer, which no amount of data will overcome. In business as in life, some truths are inconvenient . . . but they nevertheless remain true.

Shave Close

In Chapter 6, I talked about Henry David Thoreau, the nineteenth-century philosophical essayist who built a cabin on the shore of Walden Pond on acreage borrowed from his friend and mentor Ralph Waldo Emerson. Thoreau defined his life as his business, and he wanted to simplify that business, so that he could "live deep and suck out all the marrow of life" while putting "to rout all that was not life." He wanted to "shave close," focusing on the critical few while eschewing the trivial many.

For those of us who lead companies, *Walden* has this key lesson to offer: run your business *deliberately*. Focus on its essential facts, the critical few, and eschew the trivial many. Put another way, invest the organization's assets, time, and effort in what is productive rather than unproductive. As you shave even closer during the span of your business plan, go beyond Quad 4 and consider what you can do to improve the marginal and less than optimally productive aspects of the business in Quads 2 and 3. You want to get to the point where you consistently deploy 80 percent of your resources to "suck out all the marrow"—the marrow being the value created by the *critical few*—while putting "to rout all that" constitutes the *trivial many*.

Let's recap some of the basics laid out in the first eight chapters of this book. You can use 80/20 to analyze the data generated by your customers, products, sales, costs, profitability, markets, and regions to segment your product/customer revenue into quads that reveal the performance of (1) your A products/A customers, (2) B products/A customers, (3) A products/B customers, and (4) your B products/B customers. This will reveal what product/customer combinations generate roughly 80 percent of your revenue and profits. To this segment—called Quad 1, consisting of roughly 20 percent your A products/A customers—you should be allocating as close to 80 percent of your assets and effort as you can.

In the first hundred days, the organization typically concentrates on simplifying Quad 4. Having done that, executives turn to Quads 2 and 3, the simplification of which requires more thoughtful nuance. For this reason, the fine-tuning of the 80/20 process extends beyond the first hundred days and into the first full year under the new business plan. Indeed, 80/20 simplification is part of monthly and quarterly reviews that extend throughout the three to five years covered by the business plan.

Here is a quick review of the four quads of 80/20 segmentation:

- Quad 1 is often called the fort and merits about 80 percent of the company's resources.

- Quad 2 is regarded as the necessary evil. Because the B products in this quadrant are bought by A customers, providing just the right level of resources to serve this combination is necessary to keep those A customers happy, even if that means minimal profit or break-even performance.

Tune the Critical Focus

- Quad 3 products/customers consist of A products purchased by B customers. These are considered good business if run only transactionally, using few resources. This quadrant might well be a significant source of opportunistic profit.

- Quad 4 products/customers (B products purchased by B customers) typically represent a small fraction of revenue and, also typically, a loss—negative profit. The solution here is to price these products up, simplify and automate the selling process, and drop the products that create nothing but loss. This means letting the lowest-performing customers go and, in short, exiting this market.

Generally, the priority is to focus as much of your resources on serving—indeed, *overserving*—the 20 percent of A customers and the A products they buy through allocating roughly 80 percent of your resources (personnel and other assets) to them.

Simplifying Through Year 1

The first full year following the first hundred days is something of an extended test drive or shakedown cruise. Expect that things will need adjustment. Expect that things will need fixing. Expect that thinking and rethinking will be required. Don't sweat it. Just do it. It is all part of the necessary work.

You and your team should be guided by the imperative to reduce complexity in areas that are most important to the business. The most obvious simplification is reducing product offerings and/or the range of product models and variations. For example, you might decide to stop selling retro-style landline phones altogether. Or, recognizing that one model of such phones sells profitably, you might drop the variations on it and sell only what is pulling its weight and even making a profit. Be aware that simplification comes at a cost.

If you significantly reduce what you offer, you will likely lose some customers. That can feel painful, but nothing is more painful than squandering precious resources—especially personnel—on customers who buy little. A customer who costs you money and sucks resources from your high-performing quad is killing you. Let them go and be happy for both of you.

If you are applying 80/20 vigorously, you might decide that your sales team should not focus on B customers at all, except for those who buy A products (Quad 3). This does not mean that you should shut your doors to all B customers. Instead, use the dirty dozen (see Chapter 3) to change the way you serve this customer tier. Make these sales transactional rather than consultative. Make these products available online only, so that no human sales intervention is required.

For the products in Quad 4, the prescription is generally simple. Price the goods up to the point that selling these B products to B customers turns a profit. The beneficial effect of pricing up, by the way, might be produced by charging more but also by implementing one or more of the practices enumerated in the dirty dozen. Those Quad 4 sales you can make intensively transactional—automated, without the allocation of human resources or making other investments—stand a good chance of making a profit. Whatever you do to reduce Quad 4, at least some B customers will leave you. Well, the profitability of the business requires that they do. Godspeed to them.

The methods you use to de-resource Quad 4—the whole dirty dozen menu—should also be applied to Quad 3—A products purchased by B customers—but the A customers purchasing B products in Quad 2 expect some degree of sales force commitment and should receive it. Finding the balance between purely transactional sales and consultative, human-mediated sales requires thinking beyond any kneejerk or lockstep response to the 80/20 analysis.

Choose Your Tool

At the risk of becoming repetitious, the simplest tool to choose for simplification is to simplify the number of products the business offers. The A products in Quads 1 and 2 are likely immune from simplification, but the large number of products—roughly 80 percent—that produce just 20 percent of your total revenue are candidates for the simplest form of simplification. Because they create unnecessary complexity that bleeds resources away from the A products, cutting the worst-performing B products from your inventory not only reduces losses but also reduces voracious opportunity costs by freeing up more resources to serve the A-product/A-customer quad. If you thoughtlessly devote maximum resources to unprofitable products and product lines, you will cannibalize the company's performance when it comes to profiting from your best products and best customers.

Your Quad Manual

Quad 1: These are the 20 percent of A customers and 20 percent of products that generate roughly 80 percent of your revenue and even more of your profit. For this reason, both customers and products are sometimes referred to as "your 80s." Well, you know what to do with them. *Over-resource* them by reallocating some 80 percent of the resources languishing in Quad 4 to Quad 1. The quad's nickname—The Fort—says it all: *Hold The Fort!*

Quads 2–4: Look for ways to move to Quad 1 the products and customers in these quads. For most of them, this will be difficult if not impossible. But give it a try.

Quad 2: Simplify Quad 2 by reducing the number of stockkeeping units (SKUs) that represent mere variations on other SKUs.

For example, how many colors of extension cords do you want to offer? Black, white, and beige typically sell briskly. But pink, yellow, red? (*Really?*) How many variations on combination packages do you need in your inventory? How many sizes of petroleum jelly? Look to consolidate multiple SKUs into one or two or three that can be promoted up to Quad 1 territory. Dump the rest. Variety, they say, is the spice of life, so product variations can be attractive. But be granular in your tracking. Weed out the variations that are holding the category in Quad 2. Liberated, the product might just ascend into Quad 1, where the living is easy—and profitable.

Quad 3: Glance back at Quad 2, which consists of A customers buying B products. This makes Quad 2 a necessary evil because you want to keep your A customers satisfied, which is an incentive to retain the B products they demand. (Ideally, you will be able to consolidate numerous SKUs that are varieties and variations of these A-desired B products and thereby promote the remaining SKU or SKUs to Quad 1.) By contrast, Quad 3 consists of B customers who buy A products. So, here you must focus on marketing and distribution channels. These B customers generally come with higher transaction costs than their revenue earns. With Quad 3, you therefore want to do two things: First, you might find B customers in this quad who can be promoted to Quad 1 by targeting them for the sale of additional products that will increase their spend. Second, you want to reduce the cost of selling to them by partially de-resourcing Quad 3 using the dirty dozen toolbox or simply making all sales more intensively transactional. This is different from the treatment appropriate for Quad 2, where you are still selling B products, but to customers you want to over-resource so as to retain them.

Quad 4: Here are gathered your B customers buying B products. This quad has your highest transaction costs relative to earnings. The natural impulse is simply to take a hatchet to the whole cursed thing. In some cases, this might be the best option, especially if your turnaround mandate is to focus exclusively on the company's core products and core customers. In most cases, this focus is a great idea, provided it is not defined as *absolutely* exclusive. For one thing, a program that unconditionally banishes noncore customers and noncore products is likely to meet with rancorous internal opposition. Alignment, so necessary in earning the right to grow, will be difficult to achieve under these circumstances. Even more important, however, in the fullness of time—that is, the three to five years contemplated in the business plan—some noncore products might evolve into winners, even prompting a redefinition of the company's core. For instance, IBM was for most of its existence strictly a maker of calculator and computer hardware. Today, its core has expanded to encompass consulting and software-as-a-service. Conversely, Microsoft famously "put a computer on every desk and in every home"—without making a single computer, because its core business was software. Today, its line of Surface laptops is part of the company's core. Similarly, today's noncore customers can become core customers—as the company evolves.

Quad 4 should be treated primarily as territory to be aggressively simplified, but not necessarily simplified out of existence. Look closely at the customers in this quad with an eye toward simplifying the support they are given. Price up or price out products here and apply the dirty dozen tools to make the business transactional to reduce the cost of sales.

SKU-Focused Simplification

Over the first full year following the first hundred days, use 80/20 to shave off as many SKUs as possible without doing harm to your fort, Quad 1, and without inflicting serious damage to gross margin. A good rule of thumb is to hold the impact to 2–4 percent of total gross margin while reducing SKUs by 30–40 percent. Shifting customers from one product offering to another, for example, can reduce SKUs while minimizing the impact on gross margin.

You should target these items for simplification:

- Products that simply don't sell
- Low-volume products that are costly to manufacture
- Low-volume products that are costly to warehouse
- Products that differ only in packaging
- Products packaged in various quantities
- Different products that serve the same application
- Overly numerous color choices
- Obscure, little-ordered replacement parts
- Parts for products you no longer sell
- Unprofitable products stocked only because management happens to like them
- Low-selling products outside of the company's core

As for customers, consider dropping those that are the following:

- Require low-demand products
- Are beyond your geographical range
- Offer very low margin
- Make frequent small orders, which create inordinately high transaction costs

Segmenting the Entire Enterprise

Customers and products are not the only entities subject to segmentation. Entire business units, divisions, and the whole enterprise itself can be segmented. Doing this is appropriate when an enterprise, portfolio business, subsidiary, division, or other business unit demonstrates poor performance. A common scenario is when an enterprise grows non-strategically, typically through undisciplined mergers and acquisitions, so that its core is diluted by an amalgam of dissimilar businesses.

In these cases, it is not sufficient to restrict simplification to products and customers. The objective here must be to simplify the allocation of resources by rationalizing the structure of the enterprise, separating unlike businesses into smaller businesses that can better focus on high-performing areas. The benefit here is that leadership will gain the ability to track each specialized business more accurately and thereby customize dedicated resources to the needs of customer bases with similar needs. Segmenting the enterprise this way can be a highly effective alternative to simply discontinuing individual products or product lines that underperform not because there is something wrong with the products but because they get insufficient attention from the management and personnel of a business that has become too diverse and diffuse.

Segmenting the entire enterprise or one or more of its constituent businesses in this manner might save corporate leadership from making the mistake of turning their backs on potentially profitable products and potential Quad 1 customers. Making decisions affecting the structure of the business itself should begin in the first hundred days but require all of Year 1 and the entire span of years under the current business plan to fully evaluate, modify, and fine-tune.

From Panic to Profit

Chapter 11

Develop Your Talent with 70/20/10

There is no substitute for talent. Industry and all the virtues are of no avail.

—Aldous Huxley, *Point Counter-Point,* 1928

80/20, 80/20, 80/20, 70/20/10. And now you're throwing a new ratio at me? With not two but three numbers! WTF?

Relax.

80/20 is not going away, but 70/20/10 is also important, and it will help you to apply the benefits of 80/20 to how your company manages your human assets, how you cultivate and promote talent, and how you make hiring decisions. But, before we get to 70/20/10, let's go back to 80/20.

For Whom the Bell Curve Tolls

At this point in this book, it should come as no surprise that the Pareto principle is almost certainly at work on your workforce. By this I mean to tell you that roughly 20 percent of your employees drive roughly 80 percent of your revenue, your productivity, your success. The other 80 percent of your workforce? Well, it's a very good bet that they are driving just 20 percent of your truly positive results.

You know where this is going. Something like 20 percent of your people are making a critical positive impact. The remaining 80 percent have a more or less trivial impact on positive results but you *are* paying them anyway.

Is this a cruel and heartless way of looking at your workforce? Historically, I believe a lot of people have thought so. A common, seemingly imperishable, belief in the business world is that just about everything, including human performance, follows what mathematicians and statisticians call the *normal distribution* and what the rest of us refer to as the *bell curve*.

Almost all of us have grown up with the bell curve. In school, our performance was more often than not "graded on the curve," meaning on a bell curve. HR executives and others, clear up to the C-suite, who rely on the bell curve to manage their company's human assets take a leaf from educators, wittingly or unwittingly. No doubt, they sincerely believe they are modeling their management practices on mathematically provable reality. Why else would the bell curve be called the *normal* distribution. And if normal isn't reality, what is?

By way of answering this last question, consider the name a rising young politician chose for his party early in the last century. Originally, czarist Russia's rising revolutionaries, led by Vladimir Ilych Lenin, called themselves the Russian Social Democratic Labor Party (RSDLP). At the Second Party Congress in 1903, a portion of the RSDLP split off. It was at the time a minority splinter group and so became known as the Mensheviks. In Russian, the *mensheviki* are members of the minority, the *menshivintsvo*. Lenin, naturally now referred to his remaining majority as the Bolsheviks. The Russian word for majority is *bolshinstvo*, and members of the majority are thus called *bolsheviki*, Bolsheviks. Between 1903 and the October Revolution of 1917, which ended the reign of the czars, the actual numbers in each faction fluctuated wildly. In fact, the Mensheviks were often the majority party and the Bolsheviks the minority. No matter. Lenin always called his party the Bolshevik Party—literally, the Majority Party—and the rival party remained the Menshevik Party, even when it was in the majority. The label, not the numbers, became political if not mathematical reality.

And so it is with the bell curve, at least when applied to people performance and people management. The bell curve claims to
prove the reality of a bell-shaped *normal* distribution." In fact, this
is an assumption about reality, not a proof of the nature of reality
as it really is. The bell curve model is drawn on the assumption that
there are equivalent numbers of people above and below average
and that, therefore, a very small number of people will be found at
two standard deviations above and below the mean (average). (A
"standard deviation," the symbol for which is the lowercase Greek
letter sigma, σ, is a measure of how dispersed data is in relation to
the mean.)

This mathematically symmetrical and quite beautiful curve seems
to put reality up in bright neon lights:

**Your business is not from Mars but from planet
Earth, and on Earth, there are always a small number of very high performers and an equivalent
number of very low performers, with the rest of any
organization being pretty much average.**

As Josh Bersin noted in "The Myth of the Bell Curve: Look for the
Hyper-Performers" (*Forbes*, February 19, 2014), most managers base
personnel decisions in sales, for instance, on a curve anchored to
average sales per employee. If this average was $1 million/year, the
manager would plot out a bell curve accordingly (see Figure 11-1).

As Bersin explains, the curve reflects a corporate policy of "rank
and yank," in which the company is forced "to distribute raises and
performance ratings by this curve." Unfortunately, management only
assumes that actual performance (reality) is distributed in the manner illustrated by the curve. In truth, the picture compels "managers
to have a certain percentage at the top, certain percentage at the
bottom, and a large swath in the middle." The curve does not reflect

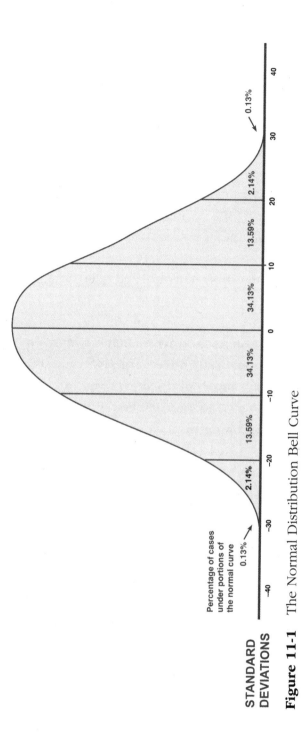

Figure 11-1 The Normal Distribution Bell Curve

reality; it imposes—by a sort of fiat—its own reality. Managers are instructed to ration high performance ratings. Think of a classroom in which performance is graded on a five-point scale, A down to F. The teacher declares that no more than 10 percent of the students in the class will receive an A and no more than 10 percent will receive an F. It follows that just 10 percent will be the winners (the scholars) and, at the other extreme of the curve, just 10 percent will be the losers (the dunces). It is possible that the whole class will be reasonably high performers or even exceptionally high performers. No matter. The curve is based on the mean, so there must be winners and losers, and the losers will be yanked—flunked out, fired.

In business, the top 10 percent might well be rewarded with the highest salaries. But these people represent a small minority. The fact is that most of the company's human assets will be found clustered in the middle, between the two extremes, and, therefore, most of the money available for salaries will go to *average* performers. The company's major investment is thus in mediocrity because the bell curve forces managers to allocate most of the company's resources not to the top 20 percent performers (per the Pareto principle) but (assuming you simply jettison the lowest 10 percent) to the remaining "average" 80 percent. This allocation of resources is blatantly nonstrategic and highly unlikely to earn any company the right to grow.

Many—perhaps most—businesses make HR decisions according to the bell curve. Yet, manifestly, it does not reflect the way the world really works. Josh Bersin cites research, based on the performance of 633,263 researchers, entertainers, politicians, and athletes, which shows that 94 percent of these groups do not follow normal distribution at all. Instead, they follow so-called power law distribution (See Ernest O'Boyle Jr. and Herman Aguinis, "The Best and the Rest: Revisiting the Norm of Normality of Individual Performance," *Personnel Psychology*, 65 (2012), 79–119).

Develop Your Talent with 70/20/10

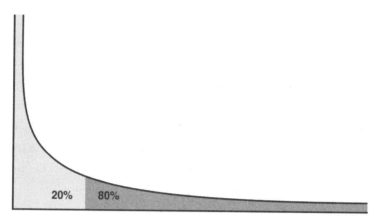

Figure 11-2 The Power Law Curve's Long Tail

Figure 11-2 shows what the power law curve looks like.

The picture of reality this presents is a small number of people who are hyper-high performers. They are at the left of the curve, which has a long tail trailing off sharply to the right. The long tail is composed of a broad range of average performers and a smaller range of lower performers.

Now, guess what the synonym for power law distribution is. Go on! *Guess!*

That's right: the Pareto curve, Pareto principle, or 80/20.

Roughly 10–15 percent of those clustered at the extreme left-hand end of the curve are hyper-high performers. They represent the highest-performing fraction of the roughly 20 percent of employees who are the company's high performers. You might want to call 5–10 percent of the high performers who don't quite make the hyper-high cut your near-hyper-high performers. Whatever you call them, all 20 percent (roughly speaking) at the far left are your A employees.

Who are they?

They are the people you want to attract, empower, develop, and retain. They are the people who do such things as innovate new products, sell the hell out of the products you have, lead great teams, and even start great companies or divisions within your company. They are the employees who drive your company's net worth to greater heights. They create value.

But what about that long tail?

Don't ignore it, don't despise it, and don't take a chainsaw to it. Just as you try to promote customers and products from Quads 2 and 3 up to Quad 1, you should look for ways to develop the near-hyper-high performers to full-on hyper-high performers, and, farther down the tail, look for employees with high potential and what Bersin calls "potential high potential." Cultivate, mentor, and challenge these groups. Doubtless, as is true of some or possibly most of the customers and products in Quad 4, there will be employees who do not fit into what your organization needs. With these, you will need to part company.

Applying 80/20 to the Talent You Have

The 80/20 principle applies not only to customers, products, business segments, and processes but also to employees. Roughly speaking—and I mean *roughly* in every sense of the word—20 percent of employees shoulder 80 percent of the productive work of the business. A more positive way of putting this is that 20 percent of employees are so-called floor leaders, that is natural leaders, who drive achievement and value. They are likely a combination of hyper-high performers, near-hyper-high performers, and potential hyper-high performers.

You can look at the entire power law curve from a glass-half-full point of view and argue that the 80 percent of lower-performing employees still show a wide range of actual performance and promising potential. Among these are almost certainly potential *near* hyper-high performers and perhaps even a smaller number of potential hyper-high performers. Even better, however, the fraction of the lower 80 percent who are truly poor performers, with little to no potential, is typically quite small. Perhaps only 20 percent of lower-performing employees cause 80 percent of the out-and-out problems in your workforce. These employees belong in Quad 4, and if their performance cannot be improved, they should be shown the door.

Segment the employees by initially identifying the 20 percent of hyper-, near-hyper, and potentially hyper-high performers. Sometimes these people are obvious by mere observation, but employees who are directly linked to profit and loss, sales, or other positions in which performance output can be readily quantified and thus ranked in formal terms of 80/20 are the most reliable candidates for inclusion in your Quad 1 personnel segment. In addition to whatever performance metrics are available, listen to feedback from colleagues. Get internal referrals. Focus on developing, rewarding, incentivizing, and training people in the top-performing segment for promotion. Position your hyper-high performers and near-hyper-high performers for promotion from within. Employees who are aware that promotion is a possibility are naturally less likely to look outside the company for opportunity.

Promotion from within is not a perk you offer employees but a business strategy that must serve the overall strategy as embodied in the company's action plan and business plan. Focus on critical positions with high turnover or high vacancy rates. Give these critical needs a high priority and invest in education and training, especially on-the-job training (OJT), to develop internal candidates for your critical roles.

After the high-performing 20 percent have been addressed, develop the skills of the remaining 80 percent. Your impulse might be to begin with the lowest performers. Resist that impulse. Identify instead those with real potential for improvement. Support them, encourage them, coach, train, and even mentor the most promising of them.

Good managers always possess the ability to delegate productively. They understand employee strengths and weaknesses and make assignments accordingly. First and foremost, they identify strengths and play to those strengths. This is the surest way to elevate performance and move employees from lower levels of performance to higher levels.

We will get into 70/20/10 in just a moment, but be aware at the outset that OJT is the most valuable and value-rich tool you have for job and career development. Accelerate OJT by investing in coaching, which is invariably more effective than classroom education. Make certain that employees are aware of available coaching programs and publicize your company's strong promote-from-within orientation. Practice internal marketing of all the available paths to promotion. Encourage your top employees to move up. Consider offering workshops in how to advance or get promoted.

Remember: what is true of customers—your best customer is the customer you already have—is true of your hyper-high-performing and near-hyper-high-performing employees. The grass might be greener on the other side of the fence or might just seem to be. Counter both the reality and the appearance of a rival firm's greener pastures by ensuring that you make yours super green with opportunity that is real, available, and worth working toward.

The 80/20 Recruiter

The grass isn't always greener somewhere other than where you happen to be. In fact, filling open positions from the talent pool you already have offers an inherent advantage. Leaders in your company already know who the high performers are. This makes them very reliable sources of referral, and, provided that the referrals are enthusiastic, it offers a high probability that moving this person up internally will produce high-performing results.

Nevertheless, positions open up that you cannot staff from internal sources. If you have no one in house with experience in field *x*, you need to look beyond your four walls. When you set out to recruit new blood, you want to closely observe the 80/20 rule. It is simple: *marshal 80 percent of your hiring and recruiting efforts to focus on the best and most important 20 percent of the talent market.* This is the strategic approach.

As Lou Adler, author of *Hire with Your Head: Using Performance-Based Hiring to Build Outstanding Diverse Teams* (4th ed.) (Wiley, 2021), points out, research consistently shows that the best candidates come from referrals. Typically, it takes interviewing ten referred candidates to find one with the potential of becoming a hyper-performer. A distant second are candidates who are sourced directly. Expect to see twenty before you find *the* one you want and need. If you devote time to writing a really compelling job posting, you might have to interview 150 candidates before you are satisfied. That's a pretty bad use of time and effort, but even worse is publishing a crappy or halfhearted posting. In such a scenario, the odds of finding the best person after a single interview are one in two hundred.

Adler notes that at a conference of some eight hundred recruiters, a speaker asked how many in the audience got their current job via referral. Two-thirds raised their hands. He cited a research project with twenty thousand respondents, of whom fewer than 20 percent reported that they would ever even think of applying for employment via a job posting. For positions in high demand, the number dropped to just 5 percent. Yet companies routinely spend 80 percent of their precious time and resources in futile attempts to improve their job-posting process. It is a fool's errand.

Your first step is obvious: stop being foolish, stop using methods proven to be futile. Instead, invest your precious time and effort in identifying great sources of referrals and start with these. Do not waste resources posting individual jobs. Minimize your use of postings by bundling related jobs in a master posting for the company. Never invite candidates to apply directly for a specific position but require instead that they submit sample work or a description of major accomplishments related to your company's needs. Reach out only to those applicants who truly excite you. This approach will garner far fewer applications because candidates will self-select before they apply. Adler believes that the modest talent pool resulting from such an appeal will have filtered out 80–90 percent of unqualified applicants. Praise be!

The talent market consists of two major groups: those people actively seeking jobs versus those already reasonably well employed who are passively open to new challenges and even new careers. It is in this latter group that the outstanding candidates are most likely to be found. Recruiters and hiring managers will need to engage with these candidates to find the ideal balance of what your company's available job requires versus the career ambitions and aspirations of candidates who do not *need* a job but want greater challenge and satisfaction. A career seeker offers greater likelihood of high potential than somebody who needs a job, any job, before the rent is due.

The Role of 70/20/10

80/20 will enable you to more accurately identify the 20 percent of employees who perform 80 percent of the most vital work in your organization. 80/20 is diagnostic. It will give you the data, but it won't tell you what to do with it. This is where 70/20/10 comes in.

The basic assumptions of 70/20/10 break down this way:

- Seventy percent of learning comes from experience, experiment, and self-reflection. In the context of the workplace, this means that 70 percent of learning a job comes from doing the job, trying different approaches to it, and reflecting on the results. This is self-coached OJT.

- Twenty percent of learning comes from working with others. This is OJT that is coached by mentors or colleagues willing (or delegated) to show the novice the ropes. Collaborative assignments—especially working under a senior employee—also provide great opportunities for learning from others.

- Ten percent—a *mere* 10 percent—of learning comes from formal educational intervention, such as coursework, classroom instruction, lectures, seminars, instructional reading, and other planned learning scenarios.

70/20/10 has many passionate advocates, who insist (and with good reason) that it is one of those rules of thumb that are simply valid, true because pragmatically useful. Critics respond that there are few formal studies to validate the assumption that 70/20/10 is even a thing. They are not wrong. The origin of 70/20/10 is a single survey of about two hundred executives who were asked to self-report how they learned to become executives. The results of the survey were reported by Michael M. Lombardo and Robert W. Edinger in their book *The Career Architect Development Planner* (Lominger, 1996). Indeed, the authors did not present a formal report of the survey but just an informal conclusion: "The odds are that development will be about 70 percent from on-the-job experiences—working on tasks and problems; about 20 percent from feedback and working around good and bad examples of the need; and 10 percent from courses and reading" (p. iv).

The critical message of 70/20/10 is less that people learn the most from being thrown into the deep end of the pool (and thus either swim or sink), but that they learn their jobs from a combination of self-coached OJT and getting and using the feedback produced by working with others. In short, it is the *sum* of the 70+20 percent that is most important, whereas the formal instruction provides a useful but not necessarily critical learning component.

The implications are obvious. Educating employees is costly—not only in the hiring of consultants and instructors but also in paying employees to engage in activities that do not directly produce revenue. Because rolling up your sleeves and actually doing the job is both more effective than formal instruction and is also directly productive of revenue, it makes sense to rely most heavily on OJT. Calling on more experienced employees to work with the novices is also a highly efficient use of labor. The new employee learns while becoming acquainted with established employees, and, as anyone who has ever been a teacher knows, instructing others is a highly effective way to improve your own knowledge and skills.

All three components of 70/20/10 are valuable, but the truly strategic approach to developing talent and teamwork while also integrating new employees into the organization is to leverage the 90 percent combination of self-learning and coached learning, which imparts knowledge and teaches skills while also getting the job done. This does not mean that the 10 percent benefit of formal education is unnecessary or wasteful, but it does not merit misallocating and thereby diluting any of the 70 + 20 percent devoted to OJT.

Strategic growth is founded on the strategic refocusing of 80 percent of the assets of the business on 20 percent of customers and products that produce 80 percent of revenue (and an even greater percentage of profit). Likewise, focusing 90 percent of human resources on self-coached and mentor-coached OJT is a far more strategic choice than investing more heavily in formal instruction that is isolated from the work at hand. The leadership of the business must design each and every workday and workflow to foster a level of OJT that creates a hyper-high-performing workforce.

Chapter 12

Thinking Is Required

In this world, if a man sits down to think, he is immediately asked if he has the headache.
—Ralph Waldo Emerson, journal, September 16, 1833

All enterprises, even the most innovative, strive at some level to become efficient creatures of habit. At some level, the aim is to transform the business into a money-making machine. Switch it on, and it knows what to do and how to do it. In fact, the objective of the first hundred days is to move the business toward money machine status. This is the mountain that the four steps of the first hundred days are designed to climb.

Step 1 is to *set a goal*: It is the executive leadership team that convenes to set this target, which is expressed in dollars, margins, and a measure of time. For example: reach $2.5 billion in revenue, have high teens margins, and $375 million in EBITDA (earnings before interest, taxes, depreciation, and amortization) by this day, five years from today. The goal is the *what*. The harder part is to figure out the *how*. Fortunately, if you dig into your wish to build a money-making machine, there is a set of four *hows* that give you a head start on reaching the goal you have set. The first *how* is to *grow*. This, in turn, implies another how. You must *earn the right to grow*. How do you do that how? *Simplify your business.*

This, of course, is another how that implies yet another. You simplify your business by applying *the 80/20 process*.

Step 2 is to *frame the strategy*: Your executive leadership team—or whatever you choose to call it—must build a strategy to achieve the goal. Framing the strategy requires assessing the current state of the business and then separating what's working from what is not. The picture that fits inside the strategic frame is a portrait of what works. Left outside of the frame are the outtakes—elements of the picture that do not work. Some of these might be capable of repair, redesign, and rehabilitation. You'll worry about that later. For now, you just set them aside so that you can focus on what is within the frame. *This* is the basis of your strategy. It is your first pass at simplification.

Step 3 is to *build the structure*: Now that you have framed what works, organize your business into segments well defined by performance so that you will be sure to focus on the customers and the products most likely to propel you to your goal.

Step 4 is to *launch the action plan*: Here you need to define the *hows* of the how: the tactics and initiatives required to execute the plan and to transform the plan into action. In the first hundred days, you strive to do something *now* that you have reason to believe will work at least more or less to move you toward your goal. You need to act *now*, so you cannot even try to imagine perfection. If you really want to make that money machine, the sooner you act, the sooner you are likely to build it. Don't wait for perfection. You will never achieve perfection. You might get close enough to call what you do perfection, but that's all. But that is pretty good.

You will, however, never get anywhere at all without acting. Action produces results. Results can be measured. What is measured can be improved. You can *imagine* a great deal without doing much of anything, but you cannot *know* anything without acting and evaluating the results. Agree to act, to observe, to assess, and to make sound, informed decisions based on measurement and evaluation of performance. You make these decisions not in the quiet of your closed-door office but right out front, where the rubber hits the road, and the results can be seen, measured, queried, and improved—continuously.

In the first hundred days, you will build the airplane as you fly it. The going might be bumpy at times, but by monitoring and evaluating performance, you will know what works and what does not work. Experience will teach you. At first, your flight will be rough, and you will be uncomfortable. The discomfort is your ally because it will motivate you to make the plane perform better and better. If you talk yourself into being satisfied too soon with too little, you will crash and burn or run out of fuel and just crash without burning.

Shampoo, Rinse, Repeat

The objectives of the first hundred days are as follows:

- To assess where you are now and where you want to be in three to five years (depending on whether you decided to create a three-year plan or a five-year plan). The future at which you are aiming is the goal your executive leadership team set for you.

- To apply 80/20 to segment and simplify your business, thereby greatly increasing the odds of reaching your goal by ensuring that you devote your greatest effort and best people to selling your best products to your best customers.

- To use your 80/20 insights with sufficient skill and thoughtfulness to over-resource the 20 percent of your customer/product combinations that produce 80 percent of your revenue and an even higher percentage of your gross profits.

- To use your 80/20 insights with sufficient skill and thoughtfulness to rationally resource the remaining three quads with the objective of promoting your lower-performing customer/product combinations upward to or toward Quad 1.

- To use your 80/20 insights with sufficient skill and thoughtfulness to prevent Quad 4 from keeping you from achieving your goal.

Do you want a money machine? The closest thing the first hundred days will give you is a sequence of actions that enable you to segment, simplify, zero-up, and grow. Examine it in Figure 12-1.

If this looks familiar to you, it should. It is identical to the four-step process that unfolded in the first hundred days. Well, not quite identical. During those first hundred days, this chart was called *the first hundred days*. During the three to five years that follow those

Figure 12-1 The Annual Strategy Management Process

first days, the chart is renamed *annual strategy management process*, and it is repeated each year.

You want to be a creature of habit? This cycle of shampoo-rinse-repeat is as close to becoming such a creature as you can get without killing your business. Although the process is the same throughout the three or five years your business plan covers, the reality in which it operates is ever-changing. The situation evolves or devolves. Your business grows or shrinks, but it never stays the same. New data is produced with every action, inaction, input, and output. And that is a bonanza for you because with each month, quarter, and year that passes, the accumulation of data enables you to use the annual strategy management process to make the strategy and its execution more productive because you know more and more about how your strategy is working through time in the real world. Even better, whereas the first hundred days were about earning the right to grow, the three or five years that follow are about actually growing. The thing is, to keep growing, you must continually earn the right to grow. And this means that even as you shampoo-rinse-repeat, thinking is required.

The Thinking That's Required

Each year of the business plan begins with a fresh situation assessment. In the first hundred days, this was an effort to understand the business in the present, albeit also within the context of its recent history and, of course, with the intention of discerning trends based on the current trajectory of the business. At the start of each full year under the business plan framed during the first hundred days, you assess the situation anew. Because you will have a growing amount of data over the coming months and years, you will be able to assess the trajectory of the business with increasing accuracy.

This assessment should be made and completed by the first monthly business review each year.

By the second monthly business review, the leadership team must evaluate the current business trajectory with the three- or five-year goal in mind. Is the present trajectory likely or unlikely to hit the target? If not, what changes need to be made? Even if the business appears to be on course, are there ways to increase the velocity of the journey toward the goal? Are there ways to even exceed the goal, to overperform?

By the quarterly review, these four questions should be answered and, at the quarterly review, management teams should be segmenting data and beginning to work on moving as many Quad 4 customer/product combinations toward Quad 1 as possible. At the same time, the performance of the business should be assessed by individual profit and loss statements (P&Ls) within each market-focused business unit. The idea is to apply 80/20 analysis not just to individual customers and SKUs but to entire business units and the markets in which they operate. Which units and markets should be allocated more resources? That is, which should be over-resourced? Conversely, which require simplification, so that they can be strategically de-resourced? De-resourcing is typically achieved by reducing the complexity of sales and fulfillment processes by transitioning consultative and other human-mediated sales practices to minimally mediated procedures and, as far as possible, to wholly automated (online) transactions.

It might take some time to execute the actions associated with simplification, but by the end of the second quarter of each year, simplification should be mostly completed. At the third quarter business review, the impact of the major simplification actions should be assessed and tweaks and adjustments made accordingly.

In the first and second quarters, while Quad 4 is being aggressively simplified and simplification actions are under way, zero-up exercises might begin. These proceed into the last couple of weeks of the second quarter and continue well into the third quarter. The objective of these exercises is to sharpen the execution of 80/20 by determining on a granular level just how extensively resources can be reallocated from lower- to higher-performing quads. The idea is to flirt with the red line without blowing your engine.

The first hundred days are dedicated to earning the right to grow. Very often, the great aim of these early days is to turn the business around—that is, to position it to start earning the right to grow. In many cases, it would be fair to describe the first hundred days as a rescue or rehabilitation mission. Once those days are passed and the business is earning the right to grow—that is, once the first full year of the business plan is under way—leadership turns toward identifying and assessing growth opportunities. This should begin midway into the second quarter and be up to speed through months two and three of that quarter and into the first month or month and a half of the third quarter. It is in the third quarter of each year that the growth opportunities should be acted on. Let the growth begin!

From Cycle to Flywheel

Four activities are carried out repeatedly during each year of the strategic management deployment of the business plan launched at the end of the first hundred days. These are segmentation, simplification, zero-up, and growth. They are a four-phase cycle that is first set into motion as a product of the first hundred days and then reiterated over the three- to five-year course over which the business plan is deployed, monitored, assessed, and accordingly modified.

The cycle was discussed in Chapter 9, but we recap it here:

- **Segmentation:** Driven by assessment of the current data, 80/20 analysis is used to segment customer/product combinations that ultimately identify profitable P&Ls within the business.

Thinking Is Required

Conversely, segmenting also identifies P&L segments that are unprofitable.

- **Simplification:** Those segments found to be unprofitable are subject to simplification. This ranges from strategic de-resourcing of marginal P&Ls to elimination of the worst-performing of them.

- **Zero-Up:** Zeroing-up is a way of forecasting the results of de-resourcing or eliminating poorly performing P&Ls and real-locating resources from them to Quad 1 segments and other segments or customer/product combinations that make a profit. The results of zero-up analysis should motivate decisive action.

- **Grow:** The first three phases of the cycle create the conditions for growth by aligning value streams to the core of the business and enabling continuous improvement based on over-resourcing the top-performing P&Ls and customer/product combinations. The object is not to invest resources in attempts to rehabilitate poorly performing segments of the business but, rather, to make the top-performing segments even more profit-able. This is achieved by over-resourcing customers in Quad 1, thereby closing any gap between customer expectations and what you deliver to them. Growth must be based on overperformance—that is, a level of performance and creation of customer satisfaction that steals away market share from the competition. Continuous improvement does not end, even when your customers are happy. Continuous improvement always has as its ultimate objective degrading or destroying the competition by starving them of market share.

Iterating and reiterating the four-phase cycle with the intention of continuous improvement with each repetition builds on the momentum of the cycle, imparting to it a flywheel effect. Business borrows the term *flywheel* from mechanical engineering. The earliest sewing machines did not have electric motors but were operated by a foot treadle, which drove a large wheel that imparted motion to a smaller wheel to which it was attached by a looped belt. The smaller wheel functioned as a pulley that ran the sewing machine. Even when the operator stopped working the treadle, the big wheel continued turning for a time, still supplying energy to the smaller wheel and, therefore, to the sewing machine. The bigger wheel was the flywheel, which acted as an energy reservoir that stored and supplied mechanical energy and transferred it to the smaller wheel. It thus enabled the sewing machine to operate more smoothly without sudden starts and stops. In business, the flywheel effect occurs when continuous improvement—incremental improvement, small wins—effectively accumulate and store energy over time, imparting to the business a momentum that seems to drive growth autonomously. That is, the cumulative effect of the incremental improvements creates its own momentum without additional external inputs. Business processes that provide continuous feedback to the actions input into the business tend to magnify and maintain performance momentum. Although working the four-phase-cycle requires some heavy lifting to overcome static inertia and get it into motion in the first hundred days, once the cycle does get going it will continue to rotate for a long time.

Flywheel Efficiency Versus the Pareto Principle

In a good mechanical flywheel system, the energy efficiency—which is the ratio of the energy output per energy input—is as high as 90 percent. This is an extraordinarily impressive energy transfer in any mechanical system.

(continued)

(continued)

> Recall that the Pareto principle—80/20—tells us that 80 percent of input is essentially wasted. Create a flywheel for your business, and your energy input/output level might be as high as 90 percent. But you will have to make a substantial investment in effort up front.

Transforming the four-phase cycle into a flywheel demands continual application of 80/20 analysis guiding action that is executed accordingly. Aligning all value streams to the core of the business goes a long way toward building the flywheel. Relentless simplification—based on 80/20 data—and the over-resourcing of the critical 20 percent of customer/product combinations will help you to create profitable P&Ls within your business. This structure is strategic and contributes to momentum. The flywheel is further enhanced by taking market share from your competition.

Why are successful companies often called unstoppable?

Because they run on the momentum of innumerable flywheels. They are juggernauts. Efficiency creates flywheels, which, in turn, drive efficiency. The assembly line innovated by Henry Ford early in the twentieth century was a great efficiency improvement over individual handwork, but men like Frederick Taylor and Frank Gilbreth bucked the status quo to show how even the assembly line could be modified to make it far more efficient.

Each year following the first hundred days requires leaders and managers to return to the initial PGOS process and not simply repeat its content but use its procedures and tools to identify where to focus and refocus current efforts to move the business from what it is doing today to what it must do tomorrow. This is essential to executing the PGOS. If execution does not proceed beyond the first hundred days, the process becomes mere hypothesis, yielding a collection of hypothetical benefits divorced from reality.

Everyone might agree that building a flywheel is a good idea, but it is often difficult to persuade an organization that "new and improved" is superior to "tried and true." One of the great attractions of the PGOS is that it is a system. It tells you what to do and shows you how to do it. This relieves collective anxieties throughout the organization and introduces a comforting sense of stability. Now, this is certainly preferable to unproductive panic and hopelessness, but the line between productive stability and destructive complacency is thin indeed. Stability easily slips into a blind reverence for the status quo. The problem with this is that business operates not in a status quo environment but a highly dynamic environment. The common organizational bias toward stability must be balanced by— and at times overbalanced by—a bias for action.

By iterating the four-step process in each year under the business plan, the PGOS addresses the organizational yearning for stability. At the same time, each iteration of the cycle requires thought, and thought—if acted on in good faith—requires a will to innovation. Each iteration of the familiar cycle is new because the data driving it is new. Use the repetitive quality of the iterated/reiterated PGOS cycle to appease if not wholly satisfy the organizational forces opposed to change. Use the ever-renewed output of the multiple iterations to create change. Do these two actions simultaneously.

Structurally, the business must learn to plan and execute multiple interacting projects. Bureaucratic siloing is deadly in a business because suboptimization is toxic. Failure to think about and act on the business as an interoperative system soon poisons the organization. Among the greatest benefits 80/20 thinking bestows on an enterprise is demonstrating—by irrefutable numbers—just how interconnected the business is. Over-resource the wrong segments, the wrong customers, the wrong products, the wrong P&Ls, and the entire business will suffer, become sick, perhaps die. Over-resource the right segments, the right customers, the right products, the right P&Ls, and it will grow.

Whatever else 80/20 does for the business, it turns on a robust tap of critically relevant information, which flows through the entire organization, overtopping any remaining silos. The revelations of 80/20 are antithetical to silos. Guided by the insights of 80/20—and prodded into action by them—the whole business will know the truth, and the truth shall set it free.

Among the greatest truths delivered by systematically repeated application of 80/20 is this: *a business can always improve*. A critical corollary to this great proposition is that individual aspects of the business can be improved, but their impact on the optimization of the business as a whole will be limited to the degree that these improvements are made piecemeal, in isolation from the organization as a whole. Each improvement must be planned and executed in the context of a thoroughly integrated business. Think in terms of all four quads, and you will build a better flywheel.

Stop Talking Change; Start Doing Projects

Change is a good idea. Change is a necessary idea. But change is just an idea. The most effective way to transform a good and necessary idea into reality is to stop *talking* about an idea and start *doing* a project. *We need to change* might be true, but *We need to do this project* will actually execute on the good and necessary idea of change. Begin by identifying urgent problems and urgent opportunities. Address both with projects.

What Is a Project?

A project is a set of actions intended to make some aspect of today better by tomorrow. The problem/opportunity, the necessary action steps toward it, the people and resources required, the timeline involved—all these need to be mapped out. All successful projects begin with the end. What is your goal? What does it look like? Answer these questions, and then work backward to map out just what is required to get from A (the present time and place) to B (the result you want the project to produce).

Managing the project requires a rough outline of actions and their order of execution. The outline should be sufficiently clear and well thought out to get you and your team moving in the right direction, but it should also be agile and resilient, capable of revision in response to emerging realities. After the outline is roughed out, you need to plot a timeline.

Chunk It

Break the project into doable chunks of work. Let's say the project is to create a brief instructional manual to improve the quality of sales calls. How will you get this produced?

1. Interview seasoned members of the sales force to identify one or more people who are able and willing to create the manual.

2. Explain the task to the chosen writer.

3. Identify (using 80/20) the top-performing salespeople.

4. Assign the writer to shadow each of these professionals on their sales calls.

5. Task the writer with making careful notes.

6. The writer should share their notes with the sales reps shadowed.

7. Edit, modify, and expand the notes based on rep feedback.

8. Based on the revised notes, create a book of best practices for use by the sales force.

9. Hire an editor (either in-house or freelance) to help the writer create a cogent sales manual.

10. Using in-house resources, publish the manual.

11. Present the manual to the sales force.

12. Solicit evaluations from the sales force.

13. Solicit additions and improvements from the sales force.

14. Monitor sales performance at regular intervals after publication of the manual.

15. Plot out the results.

16. Use the plot to assess the effectiveness of the manual.

17. The sales director and writer should meet with the sales force at regular intervals to discuss improvements, changes, additions to, and deletions from the sales manual.

18. If appropriate, the writer should be tasked with creating a new and improved edition.

19. Solicit comments on this from the sales force.

20. Repeat steps 15 and 16 using the revised version.

Planning a project can be difficult and doing so is far from an exact science. As General Dwight Eisenhower remarked, "in preparing for battle, plans are useless, but planning is indispensable." If you prefer, recall that former Heavyweight Champion Mike Tyson had the benefit of working with quite possibly the greatest boxing coach in history, Cus D'Amato. Nobody went into the ring better prepared, with more planning, and more insight than Tyson. Yet his best-known comment on strategic boxing was, "Everyone has a plan until they get punched in the mouth."

Every project must be chunked and those chunks worked into an effective sequence that is the project plan. Moreover, the project must fit within the parameters of available personnel, resources, funds, and time. Compromises might need to be made. Having committed to the project, the project manager is not necessarily committed to the plan. Thinking is required, meaning that the progress of and prospects for the project must be assessed in real time and, if necessary, adjusted to accommodate reality. The best-laid plans of mice and men are subject to change, which is far preferable to expensive failure. Newbie project leaders react with dismay or panic or anger when they are forced to change their plans. Seasoned project managers worry most when there are no objections or surprises to contend with. They feel certain they *must* be missing something.

With all its flaws and limitations, the plan gives you direction, and that is indispensable. Whatever else the plan will do for you, it provides an index against which to measure progress.

- Are you getting the resources you need?
- Are the resources producing the results you expected?
- Are the tasks enumerated in the plan accomplishing what you expected?

The answers to these questions tell you what you need to change about the plan to get closer to the results you had anticipated.

And by the way: every project needs a project manager. In many companies, project manager is a standard job title. But even if your organization has no such job description, every project must be led by someone accountable for its creation, conduct, successes, and failures.

Run Multiple Projects

Vanishingly few businesses make or sell just one product. By the same token, few businesses have the luxury of addressing one project at a time. There is truth to the cliché that warns, *When it rains, it pours.* Just as you and your organization benefit from engaging with each problem or opportunity in a systematic way rather than reacting to each in an ad hoc reinvent-the-wheel fashion, so you need to determine which projects to launch, how many to work on simultaneously, and how to prioritize and allocate resources among them. You need in particular to understand how multiple projects relate to one another, especially with respect to their dependencies. For instance, Dr. Robert Oppenheimer—a brilliant physicist but quite possibly an even better organizer—knew that if he was going to build an atomic bomb, he had to give high priority to manufacturing sufficient fissionable material to drive the chain reaction needed to create a stupendous explosion. This meant launching projects to build massive manufacturing facilities for enriching uranium and creating weapons-grade plutonium. Because time was of the essence, he launched the uranium and plutonium projects simultaneously with the intention of building two different bombs, one that used uranium, the other plutonium. Rapidly transforming the most complex, innovative, and untested theoretical physics into weapons of mass destruction capable of winning the costliest, biggest, and most universally devastating war the world had seen required running a multitude of projects in parallel. But each of *them* was planned. Indeed, the whole bomb program was called the Manhattan *Project*—not *experiment* or *program* or *activity* or *plan* or *improvisation*, but *project*. In the end, World War II was won by a successfully designed and managed project consisting of many, many projects, each built on subprojects: chunks.

Unsurprisingly, 80/20 is a valuable aid to prioritizing multiple projects. As always, the highest priority needs to be accorded those projects that are truly existential in importance. If the house is burning, put out the fire. If the boat is leaking, plug the holes. Beyond these projects, on which the immediate survival of the business depends, apply 80/20 to predict the likely impact of each subsequent candidate project. Focus on Quad 1. Narrow the universe to those roughly 20 percent of projects capable of producing 80 percent of the impacts or outcomes you need. This requires calculating the value of the input required versus the value of the output produced.

There is another factor to consider. It is usually—not invariably but usually—a good move to get on the scoreboard quickly with some easy wins. Low-hanging fruit is just as sweet as the harvest that requires a difficult climb. Quick, easy wins can bring in needed revenue and, perhaps even more important, build the confidence and lift the morale of the organization. We all need something to celebrate. 80/20 can help you to identify the easy wins—those requiring relatively little effort and few resources to realize significant benefits.

Business organizations, like athletes, get better at doing things through practice. Organizations, like people, develop muscle for certain kinds of work. Weightlifters gradually develop muscles capable of pressing heavier and heavier loads. Sprinters train muscles for short-term speed, and marathoners develop endurance muscle. The more the organization becomes accustomed to using effective systems—such as PGOS—the better it becomes at successfully managing strategic execution through the right projects run the right way at the right time and in the right sequence.

Most companies can benefit from trained project managers or at least a steering committee staffed by managers capable of making well-informed trade-offs across projects and responsible for resolving competing demands for resources on a project-by-project basis. Each project plan should lay out the business case for the project, include a work plan and timeline, specify the organization of the project team, and, of course, present a budget. The team should have a leader fully accountable for its work and responsible for reporting at reasonable intervals to the steering committee. A simple process is mandatory for tracking actual expenditures (versus budget) and the time put in by key members of the team. Reporting, however, is a responsibility that should never be permitted to grow into an obsession. Remember that the purpose of tracking a project is not to *describe* progress but to *improve* progress. The only measurements to make, record, and report are those capable of driving improvement.

Why Grow?

Measurement for the sake of measurement is a costly hobby. If you don't remember Beanie Babies, check out *The Beanie Bubble*, a 2023 film starring Zach Galifianakis, Elizabeth Banks, and Sarah Snook. It recounts the rise, rise, rise, and fall of these strategically understuffed stuffed animal character creations made of synthetic plush, PVC, and polyester fiber that were designed to be insanely collectible. Beanie Babies was one of a small fraction of collector fads that created great value for collectors. At its height, the right Beanie Baby could be flipped on eBay (a platform it effectively helped to build) for a ten-times return.

And then the bubble burst. Today, collecting Beanie Babies is a much-diminished hobby. And if you are stuck with a load of one-time high-value rarities for which you paid thousands of dollars, you now own the rotting fruits of a costly pastime.

Like Beanie Babies, measurement can become an obsession. Measurement is far from free. It has a cost in resources, effort, and personnel, and the cost in waste, the squandering of time spent on the unproductive, is even greater than what can be measured. After all, how do you calculate the true value of opportunity lost through what many rightly call analysis paralysis?

You don't raise a family for the purpose of tracking your children's growth with pencil marks on the door frame. In business, measurement should guide improvement by tracking growth and the components of (contributors to, subtractors from) growth. A truth typically held as self-evident is that all businesses are created with the intention to grow. In fact, although all businesses are organizations that engage in some sort of economic production of goods or services, only some do so chiefly to create profit. Others aim at benefiting society, making charitable contributions, advocating for some social purpose, carrying on a family tradition, supporting oneself or one's family at a subsistence level, creating a cultural or family legacy, satisfying some creative or aesthetic urge, or even just serving as a self-financing hobby.

The IRS Weighs In

The US Internal Revenue Service defines a hobby as "any activity that a person pursues because they enjoy it and with no intention of making a profit." The IRS acknowledges that "many people engage in hobby activities that turn into a source of income," but the agency insists that people invariably "operate a business with the intention of making a profit."

Philosophically, the IRS view seems to me too narrow, but it is their stated view and they have "established factors taxpayers must consider when determining whether their activity is a business or hobby":

- The taxpayer carries out activity in a businesslike manner and maintains complete and accurate books and records.

- The taxpayer puts time and effort into the activity to show they intend to make it profitable.

- The taxpayer depends on income from the activity for their livelihood.

(continued)

(continued)

- The taxpayer has personal motives for carrying out the activity such as general enjoyment or relaxation.

- The taxpayer has enough income from other sources to fund the activity.

- Losses are due to circumstances beyond the taxpayer's control or are normal for the start-up phase of their type of business.

- There is a change to methods of operation to improve profitability.

- The taxpayer and their advisor have the knowledge needed to carry out the activity as a successful business.

- The taxpayer was successful in making a profit in similar activities in the past.

- The taxpayer can expect to make a future profit from the appreciation of the assets used in the activity.

So, growth is not a universal attribute of a successful business and not the only reason people start businesses. But there is yet another attribute of a "successful" business that was celebrated by the distinguished and deservedly influential Jim Collins in two of his books, *Built to Last: Successful Habits of Visionary Companies* (with Jerry I. Porras, Harper Business, 1994) and *Good to Great: Why Some Companies Make the Leap . . . And Others Don't* (Harper Business, 2001). It is the idea that the longevity of a company is not merely a valid measure of its success but, in the end, perhaps the most important and even sovereign measure.

Personally, I don't buy the validity argument. Longevity is a legitimate yardstick of success. But it is only one measure, and in my view, is certainly not the sovereign measure. Indeed, in our era of extremely high-velocity technology and the rapid rise and fall of the markets such technologies both create and extinguish (anyone want to join me in the floppy disk business?), I suggest that the success of at least some—probably a great many—businesses should not be measured on a scale based on "built to last." As universal, that standard is outmoded.

"Good to great" is essential to building a business that is built to last. It is, however, not particularly well suited to building a business that might be a better fit for a high-velocity market-creating, market-destroying environment like ours. The PGOS approach can guide any kind of business you want to build, whether good to great and built to last or good to gone and built to sell.

The 80/20 principle is ideally suited to making and selling the right products and services for the right markets and the right customers at the right time and with the best people. I am not saying that this is the only way to apply 80/20. (It most certainly is not!) But I will argue that 80/20 persuasively invites you to think about the business itself—your business—as a product to be sold.

Doubtless, this notion is not for everyone. Some leaders/owners see themselves as sacred stewards of a sacred value legacy. That is a valid identity, but not one that is universal or sovereign. Nevertheless, for these folks, the very idea of selling their business is as unthinkable as selling their baby. This is by no means an error or delusion. It is, however, a particular sentiment, one of many and thus neither absolute nor exclusive. I have children and have never wanted to sell them. Personally, however, I have never thought of the businesses I lead or have led as my babies. They are means of growing value, and, in my view, one way of realizing that value is to increase it (over three to five years, perhaps) and sell it at a value many times higher than that at which it had been acquired. In other words, buy low, sell high.

A great advantage of this attitude—call it the *good to gone* mindset—is that running your business as if you intend to sell it compels you to grow that business, to increase all the efficiencies that enable you to take market share from the competition while minimizing the long, minimally productive tail by underserving the trivial 80 percent and overserving the critical 20 percent. The intention to sell tends to focus growth and render it urgent. It provides a target in time. It provides the choice that comes with value realized in the form of a large bag of cash. If you are so inclined, that bag will go a long way toward starting your next business. If not . . . well, take the win, and go on to whatever next chapter in life you choose.

As for me, I'm already thinking about a future book. I predict I'll call it *Good to Gone*.

Acknowledgments

I owe an extraordinary debt to those with whom I work daily and who have helped me grow into the leader that I am today. These include Genstar all-stars Rob Rutledge, Deryn Jakelev, Ben Marshall, Ray Hoglund, Mitch Aiello, Mike Hurt, David Scheer, Bill Marcum, and Jim Wisnoski as well as OTC and Arrowhead leaders, colleagues, and experts Adam McMahon, Matt Marthinson, Joe Michels, Michael Mostek, and Eric Buechele. Your unwavering encouragement and belief in my abilities sustained me throughout the writing process. Your invaluable insights have enriched the concepts and strategies presented in this book, making them more relevant and impactful. And a special thanks to Tori Brown, my assistant and mother to us all.

To my dedicated team of editors and advisors, especially my unindicted co-conspirator Alan Axelrod, thank you for your meticulous attention to detail and insightful feedback. Your expertise has polished this work and ensured its clarity and coherence.

To all the readers and supporters who have engaged with my work, provided feedback, and shared your perspectives, thank you. Your enthusiasm and constructive criticism have helped refine the ideas within these pages.

The foundation of it all is my family: my wife, Debbie Canady; my daughter Sarah De La Cruz and her husband, Nico De La Cruz; and my daughter Hannah Canady and her son, my grandson, Collin Canady. Without you, none of this would have been possible or worthwhile.

About the Author

Bill Canady is the CEO of OTC Industrial Technologies and Arrowhead Engineered Products (AEP). He has more than thirty years of experience as a global business executive.

During his time with OTC, the industrial company has grown revenues by more than 43 percent and earnings over 80 percent. OTC now has $1 billion in sales and nineteen hundred plus employees. AEP is a leading supplier of nondiscretionary, mission-critical, aftermarket replacement parts for a wide variety of vehicles and equipment and has $1.5 billion in sales with thirty-six hundred plus employees.

During his career, Bill has been responsible for leading several organizations through their most important challenges and opportunities, often in complicated regulatory, investor, and media environments. Taking the tools and techniques that he developed growing multibillion-dollar companies, he created the Profitable Growth Operating System (PGOS) and set out to help owners and operators around the world profitably grow their companies.

Bill graduated summa cum laude from Elmhurst University with a bachelor of science in business administration and received his master in business administration from the University of Chicago, Booth School of Business. He is a veteran of the United States Navy.

Index

Page numbers followed by *f* refer to figures.

budgeting *see* zero-based budgeting
"The Building of the Ship"
      (poem by Longfellow), 129
Built to Last (Collins and Porras), 222
Burger King, 174
business environment assessment, 138
business plans:
    action plans as, 139, 194
    assessments of, 207
    butterfly effect on, 175
    checklist for, 150–52
    and continuous improvement, 159
    conversion to kinetic action, 156
    cycles of, 213
    data usage in, 177
    deliberate action for, 178
    in Do-Check-Act process, 155
    80/20 framework in, 179
    in first full year, 159, 161
    in first hundred days, 122, 149–50
    and flywheels, 167, 209
    forecasts in, 137
    goals in, 5, 94, 144
    and growth, 166, 209
    in PGOS, 7
    and promotions, 194
    prophets' role in, 9
    purposes of, 156
    real-time data for, 174
    rough drafts of, 35
    scope of, 149–52
    sequencing, 153–54
    and SMART objectives, 153
    strategic assets in, 138
    strategic objectives in, 137
    urgency in, 155
    what-based, 140
    X-Matrix in, 144–51
    see also three-to-five-year
        business plans
business segments, 59–72
butterfly effect, 175–77

CAGR (compound annual growth rate),
    11

The Caine Mutiny (Wouk), 17
calls to action, 39–40
Capone, Al, 67
The Career Architect Development Plan-
    ner (Lombardo and Edinger),
    198
Carlyle, Thomas, 159
cascading, 149, 152
A Christmas Carol (Dickens), 46
Christopher Columbus, 92–97
chunking, 215–18
Churchill, Winston, 143
clarity, 41–43, 58, 108, 136
Claude Bernard, 73
close shaves, 114, 178
COGS (cost of goods sold), 49
Collins, Jim, 32, 222
command communication, 103
company culture, 16, 21, 28, 29, 100
competitive position, 126, 133, 136, 138,
    145
compound annual growth rate (CAGR),
    11
Confucious, 96
consultants, 8–10, 12–13, 15, 152, 199
continuous improvement:
    in business plans, 159
    and business's core, 116
    from Do-Check-Act process, 155
    efficiency in, 123
    feedback for, 149–50
    and flywheel effect, 211
    growth from, 210
    and natural law, 58
    practice of, 169
    rule for, 48
    visionary role in, 5–6
contractual cash requirements, 18, 37,
    101
convergent thinking, 132–35, 134*f,* 137
    see also divergent thinking
core (of a business), 116–17
core capabilities, 138
core meetings, 21–22, 26,
    104, 106–7

231

Index

employee costs, 85
employee education, 199
  see also on-the-job training (OJT)
Euclid, 59
*European Journal of Nuclear Medicine
  and Molecular Imaging,* 114
executive leadership teams (ELTs),
  21–22, 24–26
expansion, 106, 118, 123, 131, 137, 139

fear, 39, 170
fear, uncertainty, and doubt (FUD),
  40–43
Ferdinand, King, 93, 96
A Few Good Men (film), 31
Field, Marshall, 69
financial data analytics, 18, 37, 95, 97,
  101
  see also data analysis
financial forecasts, 136, 137, 139, 210
first full year (of a business):
  action plans in, 139
  business plans in, 122, 174, 177, 179,
    209
  continuous improvement during, 159
  core strengths in, 117
  objectives in, 151
  real-time management during, 159
  simplification in, 180, 185
  of strategic plans, 123, 135
  turnaround during, 25–26
  urgency during, 155, 174
  value creation in, 126
  zeroing-up after, 166
  see also three-to-five-year business
    plans
first hundred days (of a business):
  action plans in, 143, 149, 204
  adjustments during, 180
  analysis during, 121–22
  business plans in, 122, 174, 207, 209
  change acceleration during, 108, 156
  continuous improvement in, 123
  and core strengths, 116
  and flywheels, 167, 211

gap analysis in, 98
goal setting in, 95–96, 99,
  106–7, 109, 113, 161, 163
as job interview, 36
money making during, 203
objectives of, 205–7
origin of phrase, 34–35
perfection of, 139–40
progress during, 170, 212–13
projects during, 151
and right to grow, 136, 159, 161, 177,
  209
and segmenting, 186
simplification in, 174, 179, 185
situation analysis in, 146
tasks in, 151
timeline for, 159–60, 160*f*
town hall meetings during, 37
  see also three-to-five-year business
    plans
fixed costs, 73–76
  see also direct costs
flywheel effect, 167, 210–11
flywheels, 167–68, 168*f,* 209–12
Ford, Henry, 6–7, 212
the fort *see* quad 1 (the fort)
four commandments of
  visionaries, 6, 11
four-phase cycle, 209–14
four-step system, 23, 26, 33, 34, 109,
  206, 213
Frank Gilbreth, 212
Franklin, Benjamin, 113
Fredendall, Lloyd R., 20
FUD (fear, uncertainty, and doubt),
  40–43, 53, 58
future-state objectives, 98

Galifianakis, Zach, 220
gap analysis, 97–99, 99*f*
Gedankenexperiment, 75
  see also thought experiments
GM (gross margin), 49–50
goals, 91–110
  beginning processes with, 109–10

235

Index

237

Index

240

Index